BEYOND EXPECTATIONS

The Marriage You Hope For

Dr. W. Jeremie Ouedraogo

First paperback edition January 2025.

Book design by KUHN Design Group | kuhndesigngroup.com

ISBN: 979-8-9923255-0-8 (Paperback)
ISBN: 979-8-9923255-1-5 (eBook)

jeremieouedraogo.com

CONTENTS

ACKNOWLEDGMENTS

As I undertook the project of writing this book, I was profoundly influenced by countless individuals. I am eternally grateful to the Lord for His guidance and teachings, which have enriched my marriage and aided my progress in writing this book. His presence in my life has been a constant source of strength and inspiration.

I am deeply and sincerely grateful to my exceptional spouse, Mary Ouedraogo, whose unwavering love and support sustained me throughout the writing of this book. Her encouragement, guidance, prayers, and selflessness have been a constant source of strength. I extend my heartfelt appreciation to my daughters, Talia and Eliora, and my son, Hezekiah, for their patience and affection. Their understanding and support have been invaluable. I offer my profound thanks to all those who have influenced and assisted me during this project.

I am indebted beyond words to my father-in-law, Dr. Rod Ashley, whose mentorship has been outstanding in shaping this book, and to my mother-in-law, Lori Ashley, whose spiritual support has been a guiding light.

I extend heartfelt appreciation to my biological parents, Rev. Jacques Ouedraogo and my mother, Nabonswende Ouedraogo, for nurturing me, providing for my education despite financial obstacles, offering unwavering support, introducing me to Christ, and showering me with love and care. Their steadfast Christ-like demeanor and guidance have profoundly influenced my academic journey.

Additionally, I wish to express deep gratitude to the families of Snohomish Faith Church who contributed to this project. Your support and contributions have been invaluable, and I want you to know how much you are appreciated and valued.

INTRODUCTION

Welcome to a transformative journey that transcends the ordinary and reaches for the extraordinary—a journey into the heart of marriage as God intended. In this book, we seek to uncover the hidden treasures of love, selflessness, commitment, care, empathy, faith, forgiveness, understanding, shared purpose, and partnership, discovering a deep connection that surpasses even our wildest expectations. This journey is about understanding marriage and inspiring hope and transformation in your relationships. Marriage, as we will explore, has the potential to transform your life and bring about a level of fulfillment that you may not have thought possible.

As I undertook my doctoral field research project, I witnessed the struggles of numerous young married couples. These experiences, coupled with introspection in my own marriage, sparked a series of questions: How can I, as a researcher and someone deeply invested in the institution of marriage, assist married couples and their families and individuals preparing for marriage in cultivating relationships that surpass their expectations and aspirations? How can I enhance my relationship with my spouse to establish a marriage that exceeds our expectations? This personal journey of mine, filled with its own challenges and triumphs, is a testament to the fact that the path to a fulfilling marriage is not always smooth, but it is always worth it. These inquiries set me on a deeply personal path of learning and growth, a journey I am eager to share with you in this book.

We will explore the foundational principles of successful marriages, practical advice for implementing these principles, and the keys to sustaining commitment and effective communication. We will also discuss how to protect your marriage and navigate everyday challenges. This book is a source of hope, showing that transformation and fulfillment in marriage are possible and within your reach. It will ignite a sense of hope and inspiration in your journey toward a fulfilling marriage.

My journey into marriage research began during my doctoral studies. It was a quest to gather the necessary knowledge to inform my thesis. I read numerous sources, including books, articles, journals, academic dissertations, and theses, and studied the experiences of various generations of married couples. I hope the evidence I have collected and compiled throughout my research and findings will resonate with many couples, just as they did with me.

Let me break down some of the complex theories I encountered into simpler terms, equipping you with real-life advice and practical solutions to navigate the complexities of marriage. This book is designed to empower you with the tools you need to build a strong and fulfilling marriage.

Throughout this research journey, I realized the profound significance of the topic of marriage. What initially began as an academic endeavor to fulfill the requirements of my doctoral program evolved into a source of inspiration, enlightenment, direction, and personal growth. I uncovered many challenges that countless individuals encounter within the context of marriage. They yearn for their marriage to prosper, yet, sadly, numerous couples find themselves powerless as their union falls apart. This research and discovery journey has enlightened me and empowered me to share these insights with you.

For some, the regret of entering into marriage dominates. The challenges they face encompass feeling misunderstood, unheard, unloved, uncared for, differing life perspectives, infidelity, financial struggles, family or friend interference, unkindness, immaturity, unfair treatment, rejection, isolation, illness, child-rearing, infertility, spiritual warfare, and unfulfilled expectations. If you are nodding to these challenges, know you are not alone. This book offers understanding, guidance, and hope, acknowledging the everyday struggles in marriage and providing a sense of companionship in your journey.

This adventure prompted me to launch into a transformative journey to explore strategies for assisting individuals in forging authentic marriages that surpass their expectations and aspirations. It not only aided my growth as a supportive husband and father within my own marriage, but also inspired hope and possibility for all who seek to build fulfilling marriages.

Expectations form the cornerstone of many aspects of life. Marriage is often depicted as a journey to happiness, fulfillment, and companionship. Yet, for many, reality falls short of the dreams we once held. We enter into marriage with expectations—expectations shaped by our culture, our upbringing, and our own desires. But what happens when those expectations are shattered when the reality of marriage fails to meet the fantasy? This is not a sign of failure but an opportunity for growth and learning.

It's easy to become disappointed and believe our hoped-for joy is forever out of reach. But what if we dared believe that there is more? What if we could move beyond our preconceived notions of what a marriage *should* be and instead focus on what it *could* be? A partnership that exceeds our wildest dreams while remaining real, raw, and authentic.

In *Beyond Expectations: The Marriage You Hope For,* I invite you to explore the profound truths at the heart of God's design for marriage. Together, we will uncover that the love story God is writing for us is far greater than anything we could imagine.

Through the wisdom of Scripture, the guidance of the Holy Spirit, and the insights of research, we will analyze the keys to building a marriage that stands firm in the face of adversity, grows deeper with each passing year, and shines brightly as a light of hope to the world around it.

So, whether you are a newlywed beginning this adventure, a seasoned spouse navigating the ups and downs of life, or a single individual preparing for the journey ahead, know that you are not alone. The God who created the heavens and the earth is also the author of your love story and has a plan for your marriage that far surpasses anything you could ask or imagine.

Get ready to go *beyond expectations* and discover the marriage you hope for—a marriage grounded in love, fueled by faith, and filled with joy beyond measure.

PART I

THE FOUNDATION

B efore exploring the intricacies of marriage and examining its significant components, it is crucial to explore the dynamics of relationships and their inherent significance to humanity. Relationships
are key to our individual growth and what we accomplish together
as a community. Their influence is often deeper than we realize, so
it's crucial to consider this before discussing marriage.

A simple reality is at the heart of it all: we're not meant to be alone.
We're designed to build connections, and that's a big part of what
makes life meaningful. This central principle is the foundation of our
human experience, shaping the essence of who we are and how we
navigate the world around us.

In this exploration, we will analyze the profound implications
of our innate relational nature, uncovering the types of connections
that define our existence and lead to deeper understanding and fulfillment. Indeed, marriage finds its roots, evolution, and formative
influence within the broader context of relationships. Let's explore
the intrinsic relational nature with which we are designed.

CHAPTER I

UNDERSTANDING RELATIONSHIPS

WE ARE RELATIONAL BEINGS

It's deeply ingrained in our nature to form relationships for survival. Extensive evidence from fields such as psychology, sociology, and biology suggests that humans are inherently inclined towards relationships as a means to maintain mental, physical, and emotional well-being. For instance, consider the case of a person with a robust support system of friends and family. He or she is more likely to have better mental health, cope with stress effectively, and have a higher sense of self-worth than someone who is socially isolated.

Early humans relied on social groups for their very survival, as these communities provided essential protection, resource sharing, and mutual support. This reliance on social bonds enhanced their chances of survival and fostered a deep-rooted inclination to form and maintain connections. This advantage is embedded in our DNA, driving us to seek out relationships as a fundamental aspect of our existence.

Today, this drive remains as potent as ever. At a core level, our drive, aspirations, vitality, and sense of purpose are intricately linked to our relationships and connections with others. Without these human interactions, life can feel devoid of meaning and fulfillment. Our inherent need for connection is so deeply ingrained that relationships are essential for life to feel complete and significant.

Dr. Debra Umberson, Professor of Sociology at the University of Texas, and Jennifer Montez, a therapist specializing in eating disorders, trauma, PTSD, and relationships, explains the consequences of having a limited social life or nonsocial life "Social support refers to the emotionally sustaining qualities of relationships (e.g., a sense that one is loved, cared for, and listened to). Hundreds of studies establish that social support benefits mental and physical health."[1]

Humans cannot thrive without human interaction. God ingrained the need for relationships into our very being. We are created in the image of God, and this divine design highlights our inherent need for relationships. The Bible teaches that God made us for community, as seen in Genesis 2:18, where He states, "It is not good for the man to be alone; I will make a helper suitable for him." This foundational truth reflects that human well-being is deeply rooted in our interactions with others. From the beginning, God established relationships as vital for human flourishing, demonstrating that isolation contradicts His intention for us. This intentional design by God connects us to each other and a larger plan, making us feel part of something significant and unique.

---

1. Debra Umberson and Jennifer K. Montez, "Social Relationships and Health: A Flashpoint for Health Policy," *Journal of Health and Social Behavior* 51, no.1 (2010): S54-S66, doi:10.1177/0022146510383501.

The New Testament, a guiding light for believers, emphasizes the importance of love and support in our relationships. 1 John 4:7 urges us, "Dear friends, let us love one another, for love comes from God." These relationships, rooted in God's command for communal living and mutual care, are crucial for our thriving. The biblical narrative consistently shows that our sense of purpose and well-being is found in living out these relationships, underlining that our ability to flourish is deeply tied to our connections with others as designed by God.

This affirmation from the New Testament reassures us and guides us in our journey of understanding and living out the divine blueprint of relationships, which is the model of love, care, and support that God has set for us in His design for humanity. Dr. Gary Chapman insists that, "The truth is you are made for relationships. To experience the richness of loving relationships is better than anything money, fame, or professional acclaim could bring...When we love others because we value them as individuals, we experience a joy unlike any other."[2] This joy and fulfillment that loving relationships bring is a source of inspiration and hope for all of us. It's a reminder that when nurtured and cherished, our relationships can bring us immense joy and satisfaction, surpassing any material wealth or professional success.

A prominent Bible reference evidencing God creating humans as relational beings is found in Genesis 1:27-31:

> Then God said, 'Let us make mankind in our image, in
> our likeness, so that they may rule over the fish in the
> sea and the birds in the sky, over the livestock and all the

---

2. Gary Chapman, *Love as a Way of Life: Seven Keys to Transforming Every Aspect of Your Life* (Colorado Springs: WaterBrook Press, January 2000), 84.

wild animals, and over all the creatures that move along the ground.' So God created mankind in his own image, in the image of God, he created them; male and female he created them. God blessed them and said to them, 'Be fruitful and increase in number; fill the earth and subdue it. Rule over the fish in the sea and the birds in the sky and over every living creature that moves on the ground.' Then God said, 'I give you every seed-bearing plant on the face of the whole earth and every tree that has fruit with seed in it. They will be yours for food. And to all the beasts of the earth and all the birds in the sky and all the creatures that move along the ground—everything that has the breath of life in it—I give every green plant for food.' And it was so. God saw all that he had made, and it was very good. And there was evening, and there was morning—the sixth day.[3]

LIFE IS ORGANIZED WITHIN A SOCIAL SETTING

Life is organized within a social context. Life's endeavors, projects, interactions, and undertakings invariably occur within a social setting. It's impossible to strategize or devise plans outside of society. Society serves as the backdrop in which individuals interact, evolve, and lead their lives. It's challenging to envision a satisfying life devoid of human connections. This interconnectedness and interdependence of human life is a testament to the role of society in shaping our

---

3. Unless otherwise noted, all scripture references are taken from *The Holy Bible: New International Version* (North American Edition), published by Zondervan Bible Publishers and copyrighted by the International Bible Society (2011).

relationships and experiences. The following eight topics highlight the importance of how life is organized within a given societal setting.

Social Framework and Planning

Every plan or strategy we devise is inherently influenced by the social environment in which we operate. From the most personal decisions, such as choosing a career or planning a family, to broader initiatives, like starting a business or engaging in community projects, these decisions are rarely made in isolation. They are affected by social norms, cultural expectations, and our surroundings' economic and political climate. For instance, career choices are often guided by prevailing industry standards and societal values, while market demands and community support systems may shape entrepreneurial ventures.

Projects and Collaborations

Undertakings of all kinds—professional projects, academic research, or artistic endeavors—typically require collaboration and interaction. The success of such projects often depends on effective teamwork, networking, and the ability to navigate social dynamics. Input, cooperation, and feedback from others are crucial for refining ideas, solving problems, and achieving goals. For example, a scientific research project relies on the collaboration of researchers, funding from institutions, and validation from peer communities.

Interactions and Personal Growth

Interactions with others are pivotal in shaping our personal development and social identity. Relationships give us insights into ourselves and others, influencing our values, beliefs, and behaviors. Social interactions provide feedback and validation, helping us refine our self-concept and adapt to changing social contexts. Personal growth is often a product of navigating complex social landscapes, negotiating with diverse viewpoints, and learning from relational dynamics.

Societal Norms and Expectations

Society provides a framework of rules and values that guide behavior and shape our experiences. These norms significantly influence how we perceive success, define happiness, and interact with others. For example, cultural norms might dictate career aspirations, family roles, or social etiquette. The pressure to conform to these norms can inspire and constrain, significantly influencing how we pursue our goals and relate to those around us.

Social Support and Well-being

Human connections are meaningful and integral to our well-being and satisfaction. The presence of supportive relationships can significantly enhance mental health, provide emotional stability, and foster a sense of belonging. Social support systems—whether family, friends, or community networks play a crucial role in achieving personal fulfillment. Conversely, lacking social connections can lead to isolation and a diminished sense of purpose.

Cultural and Social Influences

Cultural and social contexts profoundly shape our perceptions and experiences. Cultural values, traditions, and social practices provide a lens through which we interpret the world and make sense of our experiences. These influences affect our behaviors, choices, and interactions, creating a unique social environment that impacts how we navigate various aspects of life. For instance, educational achievements might be valued differently across cultures, influencing individual aspirations and societal expectations.

Collective vs. Individual Goals

While individuals may have personal ambitions and desires, these are often intertwined with collective goals and societal objectives. The interplay between personal aspirations and societal needs can drive innovation, collaboration, and social progress. For example, public health initiatives and community development projects reflect a balance between individual contributions and collective welfare.

The Dynamic Nature of Social Settings

Social settings are not static; they evolve and transform over time, influenced by technological changes, politics, and cultural shifts. This dynamic nature necessitates our strategies and plans to adapt to the shifting social landscape. The skills to navigate and adapt to these changes are crucial for success and personal satisfaction. As Dr. Angela Sabates, a professor of psychology at Bethel University, puts it, "We are both intrinsically relational and intrinsically affiliative."[4]

Dr. Alan Fiske, a psychological anthropologist studying how natural selection, neurobiology, ontogeny, psychology, and culture jointly shape human sociality, maintains that people are fundamentally social. We generally organize our social life in terms of our relations with other people...people's intentions concerning other people are essentially sociable, and their social goals are inherently relational: People interact with others in order to construct and participate in one or another

---

4. Angela M. Sabates, *Social Psychology in Christian Perspective Exploring the Human Condition* (Westmont: InterVarsity Press, 2012), 193-194.

of the four basic types of social relationships. The relational models theory explains social life as a process of seeking, making, sustaining, repairing, adjusting, judging, construing, and sanctioning relationships. It postulates that people are oriented to relationships as such, that people generally want to relate to each other, feel committed to the basic types of relationships, regard themselves as obligated to abide by them and impose them on other people (including third parties).[5]

This confirms that humans need to be actively connected to survive—relationship matters in the eyes of God. Without connections, life would not make any sense. Humans cannot survive without any form of belonging. Belonging is what makes life itself purposeful and dynamic. Dr. Les Parrot, clinical psychologist and professor of psychology at Northwest University, and Leslie Parrot, a marriage and family therapist, explore this idea:

> Recently, a pioneering band of researchers studied the age-old mystery of what makes people happy. Their answer is not what you might expect. What appears consistently at the top of the charts is not success, wealth, achievement, good looks, or any of those enviable assets. The clear winner is relationships. Close ones. Nothing reaches so deeply into human personality, tugs so rightly, as relationship. Why? For a reason, it is only in the context of connection with others that our deepest needs can be met. Whether we like it or not, each of us has an unshakable dependence on others.[6]

---

5. Fiske, "*Structures of Social Life*."

6. Les and Leslie Parrott, Relationships: *How to Make Bad Relationships Better and Good Relationships Great* (Grand Rapids: Zondervan, 1998), 11.

Umberson and Montez add to this by stating that social ties affect mental health, physical health, health behaviors, and mortality risk. Social ties are also potential resources that can be harnessed to promote population health. Social ties should be protected as well as promoted. Social ties can likewise benefit health beyond target individuals by influencing the health of others throughout social networks. In addition, social ties have both immediate and long-term, cumulative effects on health and thus represent opportunities for short- and long-term investment in population health.[7]

In short, our lives are deeply intertwined with our social environment. Everything we do, our goals, and our relationships are influenced by this context. Society is both the stage and the script that guide how we interact, shape our experiences, and help us understand the world. This interconnectedness emphasizes the importance of human connections in creating a fulfilling and meaningful life and enlightens us about society's profound influence on our lives.

HOW SOCIETY SHAPES US

Human relationships exert a direct influence on biological development. Studies demonstrate the profound impact of social environments on shaping individuals' future characteristics. For example, children who grow up in nurturing, loving, and peaceful environments often develop qualities like sensitivity, compassion, and social skills as they grow older.

This supportive atmosphere helps them build mental stability and navigate the world more effectively. Conversely, those brought up in hostile, violent, unloving surroundings often exhibit social awkwardness, insensitivity, lack of empathy, emotional detachment, aggression,

---

7. Umberson and Montez, "Social Relationships and Health," Since you already cited them.

and, at times, social aversion, all of which highlight the detrimental effects of negative relationships.

These personal growth and development examples are informative and inspiring, motivating us to foster positive relationships. The transformative power of nurturing, loving, peaceful, and caring environments is evident in individuals' sensitivity, compassion, mental stability, and social adeptness as they mature. This emphasizes the hopeful message that positive relationships can potentially profoundly shape us.

Drs. Henry Reis, Professor of Psychology at the University of Rochester, and Andrew Collins, Professor of Child Development and Psychology at the University of Minnesota, contend that associations, often powerful ones, exist between the quality and quantity of relationships and diverse outcomes, including mortality rates, recovery from coronary heart bypass surgery, functioning of the immune system, reactions to stress, psychiatric disturbance, and life satisfaction. These effects do not appear to be artifacts of personality, temperament, behavior, or lifestyles, but instead reflect the direct influence of relationship events on biological processes.[8]

OUR THOUGHT PROCESS IS ELABORATED IN CONNECTION WITH PEOPLE, SHAPED BY SOCIETY

Our thought patterns are intricately intertwined with our interactions with others. We often conceptualize our plans, activities, relationships, careers, and educational pursuits in relation to people. This interconnection manifests in several key areas:

---

8. Harry T. Reis and W. Andrew Collins, "Relationships, Human Behavior, and Psychological Science," *Sage Journals* 3, no.6 (December 2004): 233-237, doi:10.1111/j.0963-7214.2004.00315.x.

Plans and Goals

When setting personal or professional goals, we often frame them in the context of our relationships and social environments. For instance, our ambitions might be shaped by the expectations of family members, the feedback from colleagues, or the aspirations of our social circles. The presence of others can either inspire us to aim higher or constrain our ambitions based on perceived social norms or pressures. For example, a person might pursue a particular career path not only due to personal interest but also because it aligns with family expectations or societal standards.

Activities and Hobbies

Our choice of activities and hobbies frequently reflects our social interactions and the communities we belong to. We might gravitate toward popular activities within our social groups or that facilitate bonding with others. For instance, joining a sports team or participating in a book club can be as much about social engagement as personal enjoyment. The feedback and encouragement from peers can also play a significant role in sustaining our interest in these activities.

Connections

Our relationships profoundly influence how we perceive and interact with the world, shaping our self-concept and emotional well-being. The dynamics of our personal relationships—whether with friends, family, or romantic partners shape our self-concept and emotional well-being. For example, how we handle conflicts or express affection often reflects our relational experiences. Additionally, the support or criticism from loved ones can impact our self-esteem and decision-making processes.

Careers

In the realm of careers, our thought patterns are heavily influenced by professional networks, mentors, and the organizational culture in which we operate. The guidance we receive from supervisors, the camaraderie with colleagues, and the competitive pressures within our industry can all affect our career aspirations and decisions. We might pursue specific career paths to gain approval from influential figures or align with our professional environment's expectations. This can help us navigate our career paths more effectively, knowing that our decisions are not solely based on personal interests but also on the influence of our professional relationships.

Educational Pursuits

Educational choices are often made in relation to the expectations and influences of those around us. Our decisions regarding which subjects to study, which institutions to attend, and which academic achievements to pursue are frequently influenced by the opinions of educators, family members, and peers. The desire to meet external expectations or to gain social approval can drive our educational goals, sometimes even overriding our personal interests or aptitudes.

Social Comparison and Identity Formation

Social comparison shapes our identity and thought patterns. By comparing ourselves to others, we assess our own achievements, behaviors, and worth. This process can either motivate us to strive for self-improvement or lead to feelings of inadequacy. Understanding this process can make us more self-aware and reflective, helping us constructively use social comparison for our personal growth. It's empowering to realize that these comparisons can motivate us to strive for self-improvement.

As Dr. Abraham Tesser argues, "Thinking about people is central to all of us. People are the single most important parts of our worlds…Because so much of our lives depends on other people, we have developed many strategies for thinking about them."[9]

Our interactions with others are not just peripheral to our thought processes—they are central to how we plan, act, and envision our lives. These social influences shape our goals, preferences, and perceptions, creating a complex web in which our individual thought patterns and social interactions constantly evolve in tandem.

HANDLING EMOTIONS IN RELATIONSHIPS

Emotions are an inherent aspect of human nature and are most vividly and authentically expressed within the context of relationships. Take marriage, for example—it's inherently tied to relationships. Marriage setting, dynamics, and development are intrinsically connected to emotional relationships. One can't speak of marriage outside of feelings and emotions. When we discuss marriage, we're essentially delving into emotions and sentiments, which are most apparent within the framework of relationships. Navigating emotions in relationships, especially in marriage, can be pretty complex. It's all about communication, understanding, and learning how to manage those feelings.

Emotions aren't just something we express; they're at the heart of how relationships grow and thrive. By honing our skills in expressing, regulating, and bouncing back from emotions, we can better handle the ups and downs of our relationships. This not only helps us connect on a deeper level but also leads to greater satisfaction together.

---

9. Abraham Tesser, *Advanced Social Psychology* (New York: McGraw-Hill Book Company, 1995), 152, https://www.researchgate.net/publication/267193226_Advanced_Social_Psychology.

When couples focus on building these emotional skills, they often feel more confident and capable of managing their relationships. In their explanation of relationship-specific emotions, Reis and Collins proclaim that several emotions are intrinsically relationship-specific; they are unlikely to arise outside of relationships (e.g., jealousy, maternal and romantic love, grief over loss). For most other emotions, the likelihood, intensity, and nature of expression are typically influenced by the individual's relationship with the target of the emotion. For example, a rude bus driver likely elicits a weaker and different response than a rude spouse, junior colleague, or teenaged daughter. This observation accords with the definition of emotion as a response to environmental events that have significance for personal well-being. Different relationships necessarily imply different consequences for personal well-being.[10]

CHRIST'S EMOTIONAL EXAMPLE

As previously stated, emotions are an undeniable aspect of the social fabric. Exercising control over our emotions helps prevent unwarranted embarrassment, detrimental and irrational decisions, and imprudent actions. Believers should strive to emulate Christ's flawless and pure emotional example. Jesus, our Savior, is the epitome of emotional intelligence and stability, adeptly managing His emotions.

Even as Jesus was crucified, enduring excruciating pain, mockery, and unjust treatment, He prayed for those who were responsible for His suffering. In Luke 23:34, Jesus says, "Father, forgive them, for they do not know what they are doing." This prayer reflects His profound

---

10. Reis and Collins, "Relationships, Human Behavior, and Psychological Science."

forgiveness and love despite the immense suffering He faced. In contrast to this divine example, our natural human inclination is often to seek revenge when we are wronged, hurt, rejected, or betrayed. Modern culture frequently reinforces this tendency, promoting the idea of retaliation and revenge as a justified response to harm.

However, the Bible instructs us to manage our emotions and avoid seeking vengeance. Romans 12:19 teaches, "Do not take revenge, my dear friends, but leave room for God's wrath, for it is written: 'It is mine to avenge; I will repay,' says the Lord." We are called to follow Christ's example by loving and blessing those who may not return our love, embodying a higher standard of grace and forgiveness. This approach requires maturity and self-control, as handling emotions wisely is key for effective leadership and healthy relationships.

Cultivating this skill is rare and valuable, guiding us to act following biblical principles rather than succumbing to worldly impulses. As Campbell and Bufford explain, "Christ is our model of emotional functioning not only in emotional expression, but also in the purity of His motives. He did not express emotions in a manipulative manner or with the intent of harming another person. Rather, His motives were pure, and therefore the manifestation of His emotions accomplished righteous purposes."[11]

GOD'S PURPOSE FOR RELATIONSHIPS

God never acts without purpose or significance. Everything He creates serves a specific purpose and follows a particular order (Proverbs 16:4). God's design for relationships is deeply rooted in His divine

---

11. Clark D. Campbell, and Rodger K Bufford, "A Christian Perspective on Human Emotions," *Faculty Publications - Grad School of Clinical Psychology,* Paper 90, (2012): 1-10, http://digitalcommons.georgefox.edu/gscp_fac/90.

purpose and order, reflecting His intention for Creation. Proverbs 16:4 states, "The Lord works out everything to its proper end—even the wicked for a day of disaster." This verse stresses that every element of creation, including relationships, is intentionally crafted and serves a specific purpose within God's overarching plan. Relationships are not mere coincidences but are woven into the fabric of God's Creation to fulfill His divine will. They are integral to His purpose, providing a means for His people to experience His love and to reflect His character in their interactions.

God created relationships primarily to fulfill the commandment to love one another. In John 13:34, Jesus said, "A new command I give you: Love one another. As I have loved you, so you must love one another." This command highlights that relationships are a platform for demonstrating and practicing Christ-like love. Through our interactions with others, we can embody Christ's love, which is foundational to the Christian faith. Relationships thus become a means of expressing and experiencing God's love in practical, tangible ways, reflecting His character and spreading His grace.

Moreover, God designed relationships to support and strengthen His people in their spiritual journey. Ecclesiastes 4:9-10 notes, "Two are better than one, because they have a good return for their labor: If either of them falls down, one can help the other up." This passage illustrates that relationships provide essential support and encouragement, especially in times of difficulty. By surrounding ourselves with fellow believers, we can offer and receive support, guidance, and accountability, which are crucial for spiritual growth and perseverance. Relationships are a source of strength, helping their relationship with God grow.

Relationships are also vital for fulfilling the divine mandate in

Genesis 1:28, where God says, "Be fruitful and increase in number; fill the earth and subdue it." This mandate includes establishing families and communities that work together to care for and steward God's creation. Through relationships, we engage in activities that contribute to society's well-being and advance God's kingdom on earth. By nurturing and valuing our relationships, we actively participate in God's plan for creation, fulfilling our role as caretakers and co-laborers in His work.

God entrusted humanity with the responsibility to cultivate, preserve, and multiply His creation, as outlined in Genesis 2:15. This divine mandate means that nothing in creation should be taken for granted or handled carelessly. Everything, from the smallest detail to the grandest responsibility, must be managed with the utmost care, respect, and stewardship. When God assigns you a task, whether a job, a role of leadership, or any form of responsibility, He expects you to approach it with diligence and reverence.

If you are given a management or leadership role, God desires that you fulfill your duties with the highest level of care and seriousness. This includes leading those entrusted to you with love and fairness, without any form of discrimination or partiality. Every individual under your guidance should be treated with respect and compassion, reflecting the love and justice of God. Similarly, if God blesses you with a spouse, He expects you to love and care for them selflessly and faithfully, honoring your commitment.

Moreover, when God blesses you with anything, He looks for your gratitude and a heart of thankfulness. Everything we possess, including our roles, relationships, and resources, belongs to Him. We are called to manage these gifts with joy, care, and humility, recognizing that we are stewards rather than owners. Approach every responsibility as if you will be held accountable for how you have managed it. Engage with devotion, love, and respect, knowing that all you have and do is under the Lord's watchful eye. This sense of gratitude and responsibility should guide our actions and decisions.

Young Seok Cha, the senior pastor of Michiana Korean-American Church, says, "Caring for the created world is based on love toward God, who created the earth and everything in it. God originally designed human beings to develop their characteristics and intelligence in the process of taking care of His world. There should be no separation between caring for God's world and caring for the people whom God entrusted to us. Both ministries are based on compassion and love."[12]

WE ACCOMPLISH OUR CALLS WITHIN A GIVEN SOCIETAL ORGANIZATION

We fulfill our calling within the framework of society. Upon discovering our calling, we come to understand that it's only through genuine social interaction and connections that we can effectively fulfill our purpose. Genuine social interaction involves more than just casual acquaintances; it requires deep, meaningful relationships that provide support, encouragement, and accountability. Regardless of ambition, talent, gifts, qualifications, intelligence, wealth, or extraordinary abilities, nothing remarkable can be achieved outside of genuine social interaction. Every aspiration, desire, dream, longing, pursuit, or admiration we harbor unfolds within a social context. As Jones Gregory affirms,

---

12. Young Seok Cha, "Theological and Ethical Implications of Creation Care," *Journal of Applied Christian Leadership* 6, no. 2 (2012): 88-106, https://digitalcommons.andrews.edu/jacl/vol6/iss2/72012.

God wills communion with Creation, and so creates human beings in the divine image and likeness. So human beings are created for loving communion—with God, with one another, and with the whole Creation; we are not made to live as isolated or self-enclosed individuals. Hence, we can only fulfill our purpose and destiny when we fulfill our God-given capacity to love, to live as part of the pattern of God's Creation...The deepest truth about ourselves is neither that we are self-sufficient nor that are weak, needy, and fallible; it is that we are created for communion with God, with one another, and with the whole Creation. We need God and others both to discover who and whose we are and also because it is only through our life together that we can fulfill our destiny for communion in God's Kingdom. Yet human beings have persistently rejected, and continue to reject, that communion...As a result, the musical harmony of God's self-giving communion is transmitted into the cacophony of self-asserting or self-abnegating selves unable to hear one another.[13]

Humans cannot undertake the monumental tasks of development, protection, and reproduction alone; genuine social connections are indispensable. Being naturally social is an imperative aspect of human life, a design by God for collective growth and stewardship (2 Corinthians 13:11). Without acknowledging this truth, we would struggle to care for God's creation effectively. After all, the

---

13. Jones L. Gregory, *Embodying Forgiveness: A Theological Analysis* (Grand Rapids: Wm. B.Eerdmans Publishing Co., 1995), 61.

Gospel is not shared with trees, animals, or objects but with fellow human beings.

When God calls you to a task, and every person has a calling, whether they are aware of it or not, you should cultivate relationships while joyfully fulfilling this divine assignment. A "calling" is a specific task or role God assigns to each person, unique to their individual gifts, talents, and circumstances. Relationships hold significance from God's perspective. He fashioned us for relationships—expressing love and care for one another is inherent to sharing Christ. Humans can only manifest their individual callings and purposes within a social context. While God's mission is for all humanity to steward His creation, He assigns each person a specific task (1 Corinthians 7:17). This personalized task or calling is our purpose for living.

Those who overlook this calling forfeit their reason for existence and will lead a futile, purposeless, and unhappy lives. Discovering this calling is crucial for living life (Matthew 6:33-34). Unfortunately, many chase after fleeting and meaningless pursuits in life. Their entire existence revolves around transient earthly matters. Our time on earth is fleeting. One day, each of us will give an account of our calling to our Creator.

Dr. Tony Evans asserts that when God created man in his image, He delegated to him the responsibility to care for and manage His creation. Up until that time God did all the work. He separated the water from the land, formed the light, grew the plants, created the sun and the moon, placed the stars in the sky, and made the animals. But on the sixth day, when God created man, He turned over the stewardship of the earth to the hands of men. Let's be clear: God has not turned over absolute ownership of the earth to men. But He has assigned us managerial responsibility for ruling it. God endowed men with the opportunity and responsibility to manage what He had made.[14]

A pivotal aspect of our calling is the Great Commission, as given by Jesus in Matthew 28:19-20: "Therefore go and make disciples of all nations, baptizing them in the name of the Father and of the Son and the Holy Spirit, and teaching them to obey everything I have commanded you." This command emphasizes our mission's global reach and our responsibility to share the gospel in different social contexts. The Great Commission encourages us to actively connect with various cultures and communities, showing that living out our calling means working within and across these diverse frameworks to make disciples and expand God's kingdom.

Our callings are intricately connected to our social interactions and roles within the society God has placed us in. Whether through the exercise of spiritual gifts, participation in communal responsibilities, or fulfilling the Great Commission, our purposes are realized through our engagement with others. As we live out our callings, we must recognize that effective ministry and personal fulfillment come through active involvement in the societal structures and relationships that God has established.

RELATIONSHIPS FOSTER FAMILY DEVELOPMENT

Relationships, in their transformative power, foster family development. Relationships within the family, extended family, church community, and broader society play pivotal roles in shaping the comprehensive development of individuals within the family. These connections

---

14. Tony Evans, *Kingdom Man - Bible Study Book: Every Man's Destiny, Every Woman's Dream* (Nashville: Lifeway Press, 2012), 21.

provide support and avenues for encouragement, accountability, and mutual growth, fostering an environment where families can survive, thrive, and flourish. This highlights the significance and value of our familial connections, making us appreciate them even more.

For example, parents are entrusted with the solemn responsibility of nurturing and guiding their children, instilling in them the values and principles of the Kingdom. Within the family unit's sanctuary, children learn their first lessons of love, respect, and obedience—not just to their earthly guardians but, more importantly, to their Heavenly Father. This intimate relationship with God brings profound joy and fulfillment, inspiring us to continue our spiritual journey.

R. Lang Frieder and Karen L. Fingerman are right when they contend that, at the most basic level, social ties are necessary for humans to have children and raise them. Yet, individuals' social ties persist beyond these basic functions to include a wide array of partners. As adults, we may serve multiple roles in multiple relationships. We are simultaneously romantic partners, parents of growing children, children of older parents, relatives of in-laws and siblings, neighbors, and co-workers. A myriad of relationships persists at stages of development where autonomous functioning is possible and sometimes even at high cost to the individuals involved.[15]

SOCIETIES ARE FORMED OUT OF SMALL RELATIONAL STRUCTURES

Small relational structures are the building blocks of societies. Relationships nourish, energize, and mold individuals, communities, cultures, and nations. From birth, individuals are integrated into

---

15. R. Lang Frieder, and Karen L. Fingerman, eds., Introduction, *Growing Together: Personal Relationships across the Life Span* (Cambridge: Cambridge University Press, 2004), 3, http://assets. cambridge.org/052181/3107/sample/0521813107ws.pdf.

communities, shaping their identities directly or indirectly. The world continually evolves and adapts, giving rise to new cultural and societal dynamics fostered by shared values, principles, norms, traditions, beliefs, faiths, and customs among people. As Fiske writes,

> Social relationships pervade every aspect of human life and these relationships are far more extensive, complex, and diverse (within and across societies) than those of any other species… Relationships are patterns of coordination among people; they are not properties of individuals…Although cultures and individuals vary considerably in the strength and—above all—in the forms of their sociality, all humans are deeply social by nature. Even self-interested individualism itself is a form of culturally organized interdependence in which people organize their interaction with reference to models of 'self-expression' and 'self-esteem,'—which are socially accomplished, socially displayed, and oriented to social values. Calculative, competitive models of 'success' and 'achievement' are no more natural and no more fundamental than cultural models of altruistic caring; all are socially defined and validated.[16]

Individuals who attempt to live in self-isolation often find themselves struggling with social dysfunction. We are not designed for a solitary existence; living in isolation can harm us mentally, physically, emotionally, economically, and spiritually. Human beings are

---

16. Alan Page Fiske, "Human Sociality: The Inherent Sociability of Homo Sapiens," *WordPress,* (2009): 1-10, https://alingavreliuc.files.wordpress.com/2010/10/a-fiske-human-sociality.pdf.

inherently social and cannot thrive in complete isolation. Those who detach themselves socially or avoid interaction often experience dissatisfaction, depression, and social awkwardness. Struggling with a sense of unfulfillment and disconnection, they may become risks to themselves and others.

If you consider withdrawing from human interaction and relationships, you must know there are potential adverse effects. While temporary solitude might seem appealing, you will likely appreciate the value of meaningful connections and social engagement over time. This understanding is not just important but crucial to making informed decisions about our social lives and can help us avoid the long-term emotional and psychological costs of isolation.

This reality is demonstrated in the American television series *Alone*, where contestants are isolated in the wilderness, and the last person remaining in the game wins a prize. Contestants frequently leave not due to a lack of food or shelter but because they miss human interaction. The isolation from sharing experiences, joys, and challenges with others becomes unbearable. This highlights our fundamental design for community and connection rather than solitude.

We are created for relationships and community; true fulfillment comes from engaging with others. The human experience is enriched through interaction and shared experiences, reinforcing the fact that isolation is contrary to our nature and well-being. The joy and fulfillment that come from these meaningful connections are not just sources of inspiration but also sources of hope, reminding us of the beauty of our shared humanity and the potential for profound connections.

Inga Eanes states that we are not individual and isolated brains and that our brains are linked to each other. We cannot lead healthy lives without human contact. We are genetically and evolutionarily wired to connect as children to our families, friends, and communities for survival and, ultimately, to thrive. It is through the evolutionary mirror neuronal system that a person learns empathy, which enables such connection. We have learned from research that when children are denied their internal reality through an empathetic response and the engagement of mirror neurons, the development of mental health problems can occur later on in life, including emotional and energy dysregulation.[17]

WE ARE WIRED WITH
GENETIC INTERDEPENDENCE

We are wired with genetic interdependence. As Christians, we recognize that our existence is not a mere accident of biology but a deliberate act of creation by a loving and purposeful God. Within the intricate complexity of our genetic makeup lies evidence of His divine craftsmanship. Each strand of DNA, intricately woven together, bears witness to the wisdom and creativity of our Creator.

In understanding the concept of genetic interdependence, we acknowledge that God designed us not as isolated individuals but as interconnected beings bound together by the common thread of humanity. Our genetic makeup, inherited from generations past, forms the foundation for our identities. From the color of our eyes to the texture of our hair, each aspect of our physical being reflects the shared heritage of our ancestors. Genetic interdependence is not

---

17. Inga Eanes, "Relationship as an Energetic Exchange: A Key Theory for the Nurtured Heart Approach" (MA diss., The St. Catherine University, 2019), 51, https://sophia.stkate.edu/msw_papers/867.

just about physical traits; it encompasses the essence of us as relational beings.

Embedded within our DNA are the blueprints for our relational capacities—the ability to love, empathize, and connect deeply and meaningfully. These traits, passed down through generations, form the basis for the bonds of family and community that shape our lives. Moreover, our genetic interdependence reminds us of our shared responsibility toward one another. Just as each cell in the human body relies on others for its survival and function, so are we called to recognize our interconnectedness with our fellow human beings. We are not meant to live in isolation but in community, bearing one another's burdens, sharing in each other's joys, and upholding one another in times of need.

In the context of family development, genetic interdependence reminds us of the profound impact that our relationships can have on future generations. The choices we make, the values we impart, and the love we share ripple through the fabric of our families, shaping the lives of our children and grandchildren for years to come. Just as a single thread can strengthen or weaken the fabric of a garment, so too can our actions build up or tear down the foundation of our families.

In essence, genetic interdependence reflects the sacredness of our familial bonds and reminds us of our shared heritage as children of God. When we embrace our interconnectedness with one another, we honor the divine design for relational living and pave the way for the flourishing of our families and communities. This shared heritage, as children of a loving and purposeful God, is a testament to our value and connection in His eyes, fostering a sense of unity and shared purpose.

Garth Fletcher and Margaret Clark observe that interdependence shapes everyday interaction. Interdependence patterns describe the opportunities and constraints that characterize interaction, defining the potential in interaction for congeniality, contentiousness, and exploitation. Second, interdependence shapes mental events–cognition and affect reflect our attempts to understand the meaning of interdependence situations, toward identifying appropriate action in such situations. Third, interdependence shapes relationships. Interdependence properties describe the options and limitations that characterize relationships, defining the possibilities for commitment, trust, power, and conflict. And fourth, interdependence shapes the self. People develop relatively stable preferences, motives, and behavioral tendencies as a consequence of adaptation to frequently encountered interdependence situations.[18]

CREATED TO DEVELOP INTIMATE RELATIONSHIPS WITH GOD

Our primary purpose is to cultivate intimate relationships with God. God's plan for creating and placing us on earth is to foster an intimate connection with Him (Revelation 3:20). He desires us to yearn for, love, serve, honor, desire, glorify, praise, and follow Him. Our primary purpose is to worship God (James 4:8). In the Garden of Eden, God would descend every evening to commune with Adam and Eve before their fall (Genesis 3:8), affirming that His initial intention for humanity is to be in a relationship with Him. Life lacks purpose, meaning, and fulfillment without God.

If you are a believer and fail to intentionally and daily pursue an

---

18. Garth J. O. Fletcher and Margaret S. Clark, eds., *Blackwell Handbook of Social Psychology: Interpersonal Processes: Social Influence and Comparison* (Oxford: Blackwell Publishers. Ltd., 2003), 359.

intimate relationship with the Lord Jesus, you risk becoming a "cultural Christian" or a believer without depth. A cultural Christian is someone who identifies with the Christian faith on a cultural or societal level but lacks a personal, deep-rooted relationship with God. They identify themselves with cultural norms rather than pursuing an intimate relationship with Christ. Without this close walk with God, you will not experience life in its fullness as He intended. John 10:10 states, "I have come that they may have life, and have it to the full." This promise encompasses not just eternal life but also abundant living here on earth.

God has called us and saved us for eternal life and to enjoy a prosperous, fulfilling existence on earth. This does not imply that believers are exempt from life's challenges, sickness, trials, or even death. Instead, we can experience more profound peace, calm, and joy regardless of our circumstances. Romans 15:13 affirms this: "May the God of hope fill you with all joy and peace as you trust in him, so that you may overflow with hope by the power of the Holy Spirit." Spiritual victory, the foundation of every earthly blessing, is accessible only through a profound connection with God. Without such a relationship, this abundant life remains an elusive dream rather than a lived reality. Let this promise of joy and peace fill your hearts with hope and comfort.

If you find yourself in a spiritual desert, returning to God's presence and seeking His guidance is crucial. James 4:8 encourages us, "Come near to God, and he will come near to you." A genuine relationship with God is indispensable and key to unleashing your potential, growing His Kingdom, and enjoying the fullness of life as described in Scripture. Don't let a shallow or inconsistent relationship with God prevent you from realizing your destiny. Allow the potential for growth and fulfillment that a deep relationship with God offers, and let it inspire and motivate you.

God desires a close, daily walk with you, promising victory and countless blessings from His throne of grace. As we strive for this deep connection, we align ourselves with His will and experience the abundant life He offers. As David Livermore asserts, "Our lives have meaning, purpose, and significance. We get to enjoy things in this world. The Kingdom's presence is all around us. We get a glimpse of peace, love, hope, and the goodness of God in our relationships with one another, in our personal journey with God, and in the beauty around us."[19]

Some resist their Creator, but only the foolish would do so. Disconnecting from your Creator leads to failure, ruin, and disappointment (Ephesians 5:6). Our true fulfillment as human beings is found in our relationship with God (Jeremiah 33:3). You may spend your lifetime seeking the meaning and purpose of life. Still, without God, nothing falls into place. God is the essence of our existence. We live through Him and for Him. This forms the cornerstone, the very beginning, of everything (Proverbs 9:10).

John Nepil argues that man's spiritual capacities render him capable of relationship with God, a wholly different way of relating in creation. This is the hallmark of humanity—that human beings are distinctively relational, reflecting the essence of God. Being *imago Dei* is then not a static disposition but both relational and dynamic. The more that human persons acknowledge and live according to this innate relational nature, the more fully they become themselves.[20]

---

19. David A. Livermore, *Cultural Intelligence: Improving Your CQ to Engage Our Multicultural World* (Grand Rapids: Baker Academic, 2009), 37.

20. John Nepil, "Relational Dependence in a Culture of Self-Creation: A Theological Query into the Health of the Medical World," *Linacre Q* 87, no.4 (2020): 438–443, doi: 10.1177/0024363920949785.

To sum up, the fundamental aspect is that humans are inherently relational and social creatures, relying on each other for survival, divine purpose, and personal growth. Particularly in the divinely ordained marital relationship, neither partner can experience true fulfillment without first acknowledging and embracing the fundamental truth that God establishes the marriage bond and provides relational principles that lead to utmost happiness and satisfaction when adhered to and implemented.

In the Christian understanding of marriage, the concept of being created as relational beings by God holds profound significance. It speaks to the foundational truth that humans are not meant to live in isolation but rather to exist in a relationship—with God and one another. This relational nature is constructed into the very fabric of our being, reflecting the image of a triune God who exists in perfect relationship within the Trinity. Understanding this divine purpose of marriage enlightens us and informs our approach to this sacred institution.

CHAPTER II

WHY WE
HAVE TROUBLE

Human interaction is vital, and the marriage relationship holds the utmost significance within that spectrum. Marriage offers the most profound and intimate connection that humans can experience. Couples need to regard marriage more seriously than is often the case in today's society. In our contemporary culture, the sanctity of marriage has been diminished from its intended sacred status by divergent worldviews. Biblical marriage has been distorted, compromised, and misrepresented, leading to confusion among couples. Many individuals enter into marriage without adhering to any values, much less those centered around Christ.

Many couples today enter into marriage assuming they are in love, yet they lack a proper understanding of love and its complexities. They mistake attraction and fluctuating emotions for love, lacking a firm foundation on which to construct their marriage. This misunderstanding has led to a rise in divorce rates, increased instances of cohabitation, diminished satisfaction and stability in marriages, a decline in traditional family and marital frameworks, and a significant adverse shift in social structures overall. It's important to empathize with those suffering these challenges and work towards understanding and overcoming them.

According to Avia Williamson, characteristics of a healthy marriage include honesty, transparency, trust, humility, selflessness, wisdom, love, patience, understanding, forgiveness, quality time, excellent communication, spiritual connectivity, compromise, and tenacity.[21] This reflects the type of marriage God envisioned for His children.

Nevertheless, these characteristics suffer in modern marriages. In their book *Praying Circles around Your Marriage,* Joel and Nina Schmidgall and Mark Batterson claim, "Marriages are suffering. Many young couples are experiencing high levels of hurt and disappointment in their marriage. Young marriages are desperate for hope and direction to make their commitment last. Many single men and women are taking a look at the crumbling marriages of their parents and peers and wondering if the ring is even worth it."[22]

Unfortunately, we've reached the pinnacle of divorce becoming increasingly effortless, frequently without the burden of guilt or shame. Philip Cohen states, "The General Social Survey finds that percentage of people who favor making divorce 'easier to obtain' reached record high levels for all ages in 2018 up about 20 percentage points since 2004 to 53 percent for the ages 18 to 34, 47 percent for those 35 to 54, and 39 percent for those 55 or older."[23] Emerson Eggerichs

21. Aviva B. Gafford Williamson, "The Biblical Model of Marriage in Preventing Divorce: Maintaining Healthy Relationships Among Couples" (PhD diss., Liberty University, April 2021), 110, https://digitalcommons.liberty.edu/doctoral/2977.

22. Joel and Nina Schmidgall, and Mark Batterson, *Praying Circles around Your Marriage* (Grand Rapids: Zondervan, 2019), 19.

23. Philip N. Cohen, "The Coming Divorce Decline," *Socius: Sociological Research for a Dynamic World* 5, no.1 (2019): 1-6, doi:10.1177/23780231198734.

mentions that five out of ten marriages today end in divorce because love alone is not enough.[24]

Many couples neglect thorough partner evaluation or premarital counseling before getting married, often overlooking the fact that marriage involves a lifelong commitment with significant consequences. It cannot be overstated how crucial premarital counseling and diligent preparation are before entering a marriage union. Failing to do so may lead to frustrations, dissatisfaction, ongoing conflicts, and even divorce. As Neil Anderson claims, "Only one person in some marriages is willing to go through the 'Marriage Steps.'"[25]

Before engaging in the marital journey, most individuals fail to dive into important discussions with their partner at a deeper level. These discussions encompass various topics such as beliefs, faith, family dynamics, parenting approaches, political leanings, childhood experiences, worldviews, conflict resolution strategies, anger management, expectations, financial management methods, life aspirations, family health history (including substance abuse), career and educational pursuits, and communication styles. Practical screening questions often go unasked, such as:

- What are your life core values and principles?

- How do you define the significance of marriage?

- Are our life goals and objectives aligned?

- Do our beliefs or faith align?

- What is your understanding of forgiveness?

---

24. Emerson Eggerichs, *Love & Respect: The Respect He Desperately Needs* (Brentwood: Integrity Publishers, 2004), 1.

25. Neil T. Anderson and Charles Mylander, *The Christ-Centered Marriage: Discovering and Enjoying Your Freedom in Christ Together* (Ventura: Baker Pub Group, 1997), 235.

- What approach do you propose for parenting?
- How do you define family?
- Whom do you turn to during challenges?
- What are your thoughts on divorce?
- What methods do you employ to resolve conflicts?

These inquiries can elucidate relationships' chemistry dynamics and connection through thorough screening, inquiry, earnest discussion, and meticulous examination. The absence of shared life goals, purposes, and beliefs can yield emotional distress and disappointment. Hence, it is imperative to conscientiously deliberate upon these foundational variables before engaging in the marriage journey.

COMPLEXITY AND BENEFITS OF MARRIAGE BONDS

From a scientific standpoint, marriage generally promotes more excellent mental and emotional stability, often leading to higher happiness than unmarried, separated, or divorced individuals. While most people enter marriage with the hope of experiencing joy and fulfillment, many are caught off guard by the challenges that arise. These difficulties frequently stem from a lack of understanding or preparation rather than any inherent flaw in the institution. When marriage aligns with God's design, it transforms into a source of profound blessing and genuine contentment.

Scripture offers a clear perspective on the divine design for marriage, emphasizing its inherent benefits. Proverbs 18:22 asserts, "He who finds a wife finds a good thing and obtains favor from the Lord." This verse reinforces the value of a committed marital partner as a gift and a sign of divine favor. Additionally, Proverbs 31:10-12 describes the virtuous wife as an asset of immeasurable worth, bringing protection and sustenance to her family. These biblical insights reveal that marriage enriches both partners' lives meaningfully when guided by spiritual principles.

God's design for marriage encompasses a range of blessings: mutual love, support, encouragement, protection, and joy. Contrary to the world's often skewed perceptions, the Bible presents marriage as a framework for deep and enduring companionship. In this sacred relationship, couples are meant to provide each other with emotional and financial support, sharing burdens to prevent isolation. The marriage partnership means facing life's challenges, including adversity and illness, together with a sense of unity and resilience. This spiritual and emotional companionship reinforces the strength of each individual, fostering a love that nurtures and sustains through all of life's ups and downs.

Ultimately, the blessings of marriage are extensive and cannot be fully captured in a brief discussion. Entering marriage with a positive mindset, grounded faith, and a commitment to care for and respect each other opens the door to a fulfilling and resilient relationship. The journey of marriage, aligned with its divine purpose, offers a love that endures, protects, and provides—transforming both partners and their shared lives in profound ways.

Marriage undoubtedly brings a wealth of blessings, from the joy of sharing experiences to the comfort of a lifetime beautiful companion. However, it can also be a source of significant distress and heartache for those who enter it without a deep understanding and careful preparation. Many individuals step into marital commitments with high hopes, only to find themselves grappling with profound emotional pain and disappointment. This often stems from a superficial grasp of what marriage truly entails and a lack of genuine effort to understand its deeper significance.

When people approach marriage without fully appreciating its complexities and responsibilities, they may find themselves unprepared for the challenges that arise. This lack of preparation can lead to conflicts, misunderstandings, and unmet expectations, inflicting lasting wounds. The essence of marriage requires more than just a legal or ceremonial bond; it demands a committed effort to nurture and grow the relationship. Without this intentionality, the relationship can suffer, leaving both partners struggling to reconcile their ideals with their reality.

If marriages today were more closely aligned with their original purpose as intended by God, they would likely be more fulfilling and resilient. The divine vision for marriage encompasses companionship and a profound partnership based on mutual respect, love, and understanding. By returning to this foundational purpose and investing the necessary effort into comprehending and preparing for the journey, individuals can cultivate marriages that are not only enduring but also enriching.

MARRIAGE REFLECTS
CHRIST'S LOVE FOR THE CHURCH

The marriage union can exemplify Christ's profound love for the Church, symbolizing His relationship with His bride. Ephesians 5:25-27 illustrates this divine parallel: "Husbands, love your wives, just as Christ loved the church and gave Himself up for her, to make her holy, cleansing her by the washing with water through the word, and to present her to Himself as a radiant church, without stain or wrinkle or any other blemish, but holy and blameless."

This passage stresses the depth of sacrificial love that Christ demonstrates, which is meant to be mirrored in the marital relationship. Just as Christ's commitment to the Church is characterized by selflessness and devotion, so should the love between husband and wife reflect this divine standard. Therefore, the marriage union becomes a living testament to the Gospel's message, portraying the intimate and unbreakable bond believers are called to have with Christ.

God desires us to engage in a close and intimate connection with His Son and Him daily, serving as the cornerstone of the Gospel. Its beauty emanates from its relational essence. The Gospel aims for believers to cultivate genuine relationships with Christ, with the celebration extending into eternity, where we will rejoice with Him forever. Thus, marriage holds a sacred, profound, majestic, and divine significance. It elevates the marital bond to a higher level of sanctity and warrants our utmost reverence and respect. To defile it would be sacrilege.

In Genesis 2:24, we read, "That is why a man leaves his father and mother and is united to his wife, and they become one flesh." This unity signifies physical togetherness and a spiritual and emotional bond that mirrors the relationship between Christ and His Church. The sacredness of this union elevates it to a realm of divine significance, where each partner is called to embody the same grace, patience, and unconditional love that Christ extends to His followers. Thus, marriage is not merely a social contract but a divine covenant reflecting Christ's eternal and unwavering love.

Adam and Eve's creation and union in the Garden of Eden highlight the importance of companionship in marriage. When God created Eve and presented her to Adam, He established the foundational relationship of marriage, characterized by mutual support and partnership. Genesis 2:18 states, "The LORD God said, 'It is not good for the man to be alone. I will make a helper suitable for him.'" Adam's immediate response to Eve's presence was profound joy and recognition of the completeness she brought into his life. Their relationship exemplified the deep sense of fulfillment and connection that marriage is meant to provide, reinforcing the notion that companionship and mutual support are integral to the marital bond.

In the context of today's marriages, this biblical model serves as a reminder of the profound responsibility and privilege that comes with the marital relationship. Couples are called to reflect Christ's love in daily interactions, striving to build a nurturing, supportive, and spiritually enriching relationship. This involves living out the principles of forgiveness, patience, and sacrificial love that Christ demonstrated. When marriages are grounded in these biblical values, they strengthen the relationship between husband and wife and serve as a powerful witness to Christ's love for the Church.

Therefore, marriage must be approached with the utmost reverence and care, recognizing its divine significance as a reflection of Christ's love. To uphold the sanctity of marriage, couples must continuously seek to embody the virtues outlined in Scripture, ensuring that their relationship honors God and mirrors the divine love He has for His Church. By doing so, they participate in a sacred covenant that transcends earthly understanding and points to the eternal joy and unity found in Christ. Neil Anderson affirms, "Relationships are the heart of life and the relationship between the male and the female is the earthly expression of the relationship between God and humankind."[26]

---

26. Anderson and Mylander, *The Christ-Centered Marriage*, 26.

THE DIVINE INTENTIONS
BEHIND MARRIAGE

The divine intentions behind marriage reveal that a deep, abiding relationship with God profoundly influences the health of marital relationships. When individuals are spiritually connected to God, their interactions with their spouses tend to be more positive and robust. This spiritual alignment is necessary for maintaining harmony in marriage. James 4:8 encourages, "Come near to God, and he will come near to you." Couples can better address conflicts and realign their hearts and actions by seeking closeness with God, ensuring that divine principles rather than selfish desires guide their behavior.

Persistent conflicts in marriage often signal the need for personal and spiritual introspection. If issues with your spouse are ongoing, it may be beneficial to evaluate your own spiritual state. 2 Corinthians 13:5 advises, "Examine yourselves to see whether you are in the faith; test yourselves." This self-examination helps ensure that personal motives and attitudes are not hindering the relationship.

By addressing any internal spiritual conflicts and realigning with God's will, couples can restore peace and improve their marital bond. As Anderson attests, "I am tempted to say to many struggling couples, forget your marriage; you are so torn up on the inside that you probably couldn't get along with your dog right now. But if you are willing to resolve your personal and spiritual conflicts first and get radically right with God, then there is hope for your marriage."[27]

The essence of marriage involves self-giving and a commitment to the other's well-being. This principle emphasizes that marital partners should prioritize each other's needs and invest in each other's happiness. It involves forgiving one another and working towards

---

27. Ibid, 17.

restoration when conflicts arise, ensuring that love remains steadfast and supportive.

Understanding the divine intentions behind marriage enriches the relationship and aligns it with God's design. Marriage is meant to emulate God's love, marked by selflessness, commitment, and spiritual unity. By nurturing a close relationship with God and reflecting His love in your marriage, you foster a deeper, more fulfilling bond with your spouse. Addressing personal and spiritual conflicts, embracing self-giving love, and remaining committed to each other's well-being ensure that your marriage remains a true testament to the divine purpose and grace inherent in God's plan for relationships

THE POWER OF SELFLESSNESS AND ACCOUNTABILITY IN MARRIAGE

Loving involves selflessly caring for one's spouse, a commitment that requires the elimination of selfishness. In marriage, selfishness is a significant obstacle to genuinely loving and pleasing your partner. The Bible emphasizes that love is not about personal gratification but about serving and valuing the other. Philippians 2:3-4 instructs, "Do nothing out of selfish ambition or vain conceit. Rather, in humility, value others above yourselves, not looking to your own interests but each of you to the interests of the others." This passage highlights that genuine love requires setting aside personal desires to focus on the needs and well-being of one's spouse.

Selfishness, if left unchecked, can profoundly disrupt the harmony of a marriage, leading to conflict and resentment. When each partner prioritizes his or her own needs and preferences over those of the spouse, it fosters an environment of discord. James 3:16 states, "For where you have envy and selfish ambition, there you find disorder and

every evil practice." This verse reinforces that selfish ambitions create chaos and hinder the growth of a loving, supportive relationship.
Couples who focus on their own interests rather than their partner's
needs often find their marriage strained and their connection weakened.

Addressing selfishness in marriage involves embracing accountability and responsibility. Each spouse has specific roles and duties that
contribute to the health of the marriage and household. The importance of mutual accountability extends to every aspect of marriage.
Inconsistent adherence to agreed-upon principles or behaviors can
undermine trust and create friction.

Consistency in upholding responsibilities and respecting boundaries strengthens the marital bond and fosters trust. Proverbs 27:17
notes, "As iron sharpens iron, so one person sharpens another." This
principle highlights the need for both partners to support and hold
each other accountable, refining their relationship through mutual
effort and integrity. Upholding mutual accountability is not just beneficial, it's necessary for a strong and resilient marriage.

Marriage requires continuous effort and mutual support to maintain its focus and purpose. Ecclesiastes 4:9 states, "Two are better
than one because they have a good return for their labor." This verse
stresses the necessity of working together towards shared goals and
mutual growth. Selfishness disrupts this cooperative effort, leading
to marital strain. Couples must remain dedicated to their shared values and goals, addressing issues with humility and commitment to
each other's well-being.

During my doctoral research in building godly marriages, I asked
participants about their intentions regarding applying the training's
insights. A predominant focus emerged on cultivating selflessness in
their relational interactions with spouses, as they recognized selfishness

as a barrier to relational flourishing. Central to their reflections was the emphasis on the intentional cultivation of selflessness.

I also asked about the critical aspects of the training. Many participants highlighted communication and selflessness. Some emphasized selflessness, compromise, communication, and empathy, asserting that genuine selflessness is imperative for success. Another participant underlined the significance of true selflessness.

Cristina Emrich holds that marital satisfaction may be differently impacted when spouses manifest forgiveness, love, selflessness, and commitment in reverence to God for the sake of the marital partner. The intrinsically motivated spouses, for whom religious practice determines their sense of self and ideals, experience more positive outcomes and better mental health than extrinsically motivated spouses.[28]

A loving and fulfilling marriage is grounded in selflessness and accountability. By prioritizing each other's needs, embracing defined roles, and working collaboratively towards common goals, couples uphold the sanctity and strength of their relationship. Marriage, as designed by God, flourishes when both partners are committed to loving each other unconditionally and maintaining mutual respect and responsibility. Couples can navigate challenges and build a resilient, deeply fulfilling partnership through such dedication.

COMMUNICATING WITH GOD DAILY STRENGTHENS MARRIAGE UNITY

Consistent daily communication with God is vital for strengthening the unity of a marriage. When couples engage in regular, united

---

28. Cristina Sanda Emrich, "Spouses' Scriptural Beliefs, the Faithfulness of Relationship with God, and Marital Satisfaction" (EdD diss., Liberty University, 2022), 19, https://digitalcommons. liberty.edu/doctoral/3725.

prayer, they build a spiritual foundation that protects their relationship from external and internal adversities. In Ecclesiastes 4:12, it is written, "Though one may be overpowered, two can defend themselves. A cord of three strands is not quickly broken." By inviting God into their marriage through prayer, couples fortify themselves against the enemy's schemes and nurture a strong, supportive relationship with both God and each other. This commitment to prayer enhances their connection and provides divine guidance and protection.

Each partner should cultivate a personal prayer life, bringing their own needs and the needs of their spouse before God. Philippians 4:6 instructs us, "Do not be anxious about anything, but in every situation, by prayer and petition, with thanksgiving, present your requests to God." This practice allows individuals to seek God's intervention and support for their marriage, fostering a sense of spiritual alignment and mutual support. Once each partner is engaged in prayer life, establishing a shared family prayer routine further strengthens their bond and reinforces their collective commitment to God's guidance.

Research indicates that couples who earnestly and sincerely pray together experience lower rates of divorce and infidelity. James 5:16 says, "The prayer of a righteous person is powerful and effective." This divine support is crucial, as it helps couples navigate challenges and maintain fidelity through God's grace. Praying together ensures that couples rely on more than just their strength; they trust God's ability to sustain and support their relationship. By prioritizing prayer, couples can experience extraordinary breakthroughs and divine favor, reflecting that God never abandons those who earnestly seek Him.

Furthermore, prayer plays a critical role in addressing and alleviating marital burdens. These burdens include financial stress, communication issues, parenting challenges, and personal struggles. 1 Peter

5:7 encourages us to "Cast all your anxiety on [God] because he cares for you." Bringing these worries and concerns before God helps shift the focus from marital conflicts to divine intervention, reinforcing the understanding that the true adversary is not the spouse but the spiritual forces opposed to marital unity. Recognizing the power of prayer to change circumstances and bring about resolution is fundamental for maintaining a strong and resilient marriage.

This is because as they pray together, God hears, answers, sustains, supports, and protects them so they will not fail. It is not because of their strength and skills. God never forsakes nor abandons the righteous. He cares for those who seek Him daily. Don't put prayer on your back burner. Make prayer your top priority, and you will experience an extraordinary breakthrough in your marriage. God will show up and show you a divine favor beyond your expectations.

The Schmidgalls and Batterson suggest that the greatest relationship decision deserves the greatest investment. Through prayer, God can give you new eyes for your spouse. Through prayer, God can rekindle romance. Through prayer, God can align vision, overcome pain and resentment, and reenergize your friendship. The richness of your marriage will be determined by how frequently and fervently God is invited into your relationship.[29]

In short, the richness of marriage is deeply influenced by the frequency and fervency with which couples invite God into their relationship. Through prayer, God can offer new perspectives on each other, rekindle romance, and heal wounds. When approached with a prayerful attitude, marriage becomes a testament to God's ability to transform and enrich lives. As couples remain faithful in prayer,

---

29. Joel and Nina Schmidgall and Mark Batterson, *Praying Circles around Your Marriage*, 20.

they foster a deeper, more satisfying connection, reflecting the divine purpose for their union. Marital success and satisfaction are often directly tied to how consistently and earnestly couples seek God's presence and guidance in their daily lives.

MARRYING FOR NOBLE REASONS IS WISE

Marrying for noble and well-considered reasons is critical to establishing a solid and fulfilling relationship. When individuals enter marriage with misguided motives, such as convenience, societal pressure, or fear of loneliness, they often face a rocky and unstable foundation. This shaky start can lead to disappointment, frustration, and, ultimately, a breakdown in the relationship.

For instance, marrying because of an unplanned pregnancy, social pressure, or financial security rather than genuine love and commitment frequently results in dissatisfaction. Such motivations lack the depth and stability needed to sustain a lifelong partnership, which the Bible describes as a union built on true love, respect, and a shared commitment to God's design.

Marriage, as described in Scripture, is not merely about fulfilling societal expectations or personal convenience. The Bible stresses that marriage is a sacred and deep commitment requiring more than just superficial motives. Unfortunately, many approach marriage without fully understanding this depth, leading to potential pitfalls. Churches and spiritual leaders are crucial in guiding couples toward building spiritually grounded and resilient marriages. Many couples underestimate the weight of this commitment, failing to grasp the seriousness of entering into such a lifelong covenant.

Research and experience confirm that poor reasons for marriage can lead to trouble. Marrying quickly after a breakup, out of rebellion against one's parents, or due to loneliness often leads to difficulties. These motivations do not provide a strong foundation for a lasting relationship. Moreover, entering marriage under social pressure or out of guilt can also undermine the relationship's stability. The Bible calls for marriages based on love, mutual respect, and commitment rather than external pressures or fleeting emotions. A union founded on such unstable reasons is unlikely to endure the trials and challenges that all marriages inevitably face.

In our culture, the allure of romance can often overshadow the more profound aspects of marital commitment. Initially, romance may seem like the ultimate goal, but it is not a sufficient basis for a lasting marriage. As Tommy Nelson points out in *The Book of Romance*, in our culture, we too often become consumed with the heady emotion called romance. As a result, very quickly after marriage, we may find that the romance evaporates to reveal two very flawed persons in a difficult world. When we discover that the bright and happy romance has devolved into the drudgery of daily living, and, much to our dismay, we discover that our spouses have a shortage of character and virtue, we become discouraged and deeply frustrated. At that point, we too often become divorced before the ink on the marriage license has dried. We are a nation of people quick to fall into romance, and then later, quick to bail out of commitment.[30]

Entering into marriage requires thoughtful preparation and a deep understanding of its responsibilities and principles. This preparation involves more than just planning a wedding; it means engaging in prayer, reflection, and education about the true nature of marital

---

30. Tommy Nelson, *The Book of Romance: What Solomon Says about Love, Sex, and Intimacy* (Nashville: Thomas Nelson, Inc., 1998), 2.

commitment. Understanding the meaning and mission of marriage helps couples approach their union with a clear mindset and realistic expectations. Practical steps such as pre-marital counseling, financial planning, and discussing roles and responsibilities can equip individuals to face the challenges of marriage with a more resilient and informed perspective.

Ultimately, a marriage grounded in noble reasons and a clear understanding of its purpose can thrive despite difficulties. By aligning with the biblical vision of marriage—characterized by love, mutual support, and a commitment to growth—couples can build a strong foundation that endures through the trials of life. Embracing this depth and commitment prepares individuals to handle the complexities of marriage with grace and perseverance, ensuring that their union is fulfilling but also resilient and lasting.

Saying "yes" at the altar requires planning, prayer, strategizing, and understanding the meaning, responsibility, foundation, mission, and principles of marriage before the big commitment. Understanding these things does not lessen the challenges you will face when you marry; however, they prepare you to meet them with a ready mindset and adjusted expectations.

VULNERABILITY HELPS YOU GROW

Embracing vulnerability fosters personal growth. Marriage serves as a union where both partners delve into the humanity of one another and themselves, including their emotions, desires, weaknesses, fears, doubts, and overall vulnerabilities. Sharing vulnerabilities with your spouse isn't a sign of weakness; it reflects maturity to openly and honestly expose oneself. It entails consciously and openly divulging deep emotions, fears, and desires to foster transparency in the relationship.

I understand that opening up to someone can yield both positive and negative outcomes. During conflicts, a less mature spouse might exploit your vulnerability; however, cultivating vulnerability skills enables your partner to reciprocate, enhancing psychological intimacy.

Moreover, vulnerability enhances interpersonal communication abilities and strengthens the bond of your marriage. It fosters greater intimacy and trust between partners, expanding the depth of your relationship. Neglecting vulnerability may result in distance, doubt, apprehension, worry, and resentment within your marriage. Chris Schroeder says, "Marriage is impressive because it makes us vulnerable like nothing else in our body, soul, and spirit. A marriage can be strong when the couple can be completely vulnerable in every area without shame or fear."[31]

EMBRACING YOUR DIFFERENCES
SUSTAINS YOUR MARRIAGE BOND

Acknowledging and embracing your differences contributes to improving your marriage. Individuals naturally possess unique traits; likewise, each marriage has its own distinct characteristics. Yet, understanding how to cherish and honor these differences with love and compassion is vital for safeguarding your marital bond. Asserting your viewpoint over your spouse's reflects selfishness. Take the time to comprehend your spouse's background and perspective, cultivating empathy and adaptability in your relationship.

Amberly Lambertsen, at the *A Prioritized Marriage* blog, claims that differences can make your marriage better if you embrace them in marriage and view them as strengths! Having differing opinions,

---

31. Chris Schroeder, "Pastoral Counseling Marriage Ministry" (DMin diss., Liberty University, April 20, 2022), 27, https://digitalcommons.liberty.edu/doctoral/3495.

unique interests, and your own individual tastes, in fact, makes your partnership that much greater! Your differences help maintain balance in your home and turn the two of you into a powerhouse couple. The key to making this work is embracing your differences and recognizing their ability to do good things for your marriage and your family.[32]

Couples should remain aware of the potential for conflict arising from differences in attitude, perspective, culture, beliefs, desires, personality, needs, and gender. Cultivating openness, empathy, and respect establishes a foundation for deeper mutual understanding.

AVOID DEPRIVING YOUR SPOUSE OF SEXUAL INTIMACY

Do not withhold sexual intimacy from your spouse. To protect him or her from feelings of rejection, disrespect, infidelity, emotional pain, resentment, and diminished self-esteem, it's pivotal to maintain open communication and prioritize physical connection. Deliberately withholding sexual intimacy can cause significant harm, eroding trust, confidence, and intimacy within your marriage. Sexual intimacy is not solely about self-satisfaction or dominance, and it should never be used as a tool for manipulation, coercion, punishment, or any form of cruelty. Instead, it should be approached with love, respect, and mutual fulfillment.

The Bible places great importance on the marital relationship and the need for mutual respect and care in every aspect, including sexual intimacy. 1 Corinthians 7:3-4 commands, "The husband should fulfill his marital duty to his wife, and likewise the wife to her husband. The

---

32. Amberly Lambertsen, "Why You Should Embrace the Differences in Your Marriage," *A Prioritized Marriage Blog*, January 23, 2018, Accessed April 4, 2024, https://aprioritizedmarriage. com/blog/embrace-the-differences-in-your-marriage/.

wife does not have authority over her own body but yields it to her husband. In the same way, the husband does not have authority over his own body but yields it to his wife." This passage highlights that sexual intimacy is a mutual obligation in marriage and is central to maintaining the unity and strength of the marital bond. Withholding intimacy can lead to feelings of rejection and hurt, undermining the trust and emotional connection that are crucial for a healthy relationship.

The decision to withhold sexual intimacy can have serious repercussions, contributing to emotional pain and potentially leading to resentment and diminished self-esteem. Proverbs 5:18-19 provides guidance on cherishing this aspect of marriage: "May your fountain be blessed, and may you rejoice in the wife of your youth. A loving doe, a graceful deer—may her breasts satisfy you always, may you ever be intoxicated with her love." This encouragement emphasizes the significance of sexual intimacy in fostering joy and fulfillment within marriage. When partners do not engage in this intimate aspect of their relationship, it can create a void that affects both emotional well-being and overall marital satisfaction.

Sexual intimacy should never be used as a tool for manipulation or punishment. Ephesians 4:26-27 advises, "In your anger do not sin: Do not let the sun go down while you are still angry, and do not give the devil a foothold." Using sexual intimacy as a means of control or as a weapon in times of conflict is contrary to God's design for marriage and can lead to severe relational damage. Instead, it should be approached with love and respect, reflecting a mutual commitment to each other's needs and desires. This is the biblical principle of selfless love and service within marriage (1 Corinthians 13:4-7).

Maintaining open communication about sexual needs and desires is crucial in preventing misunderstandings and preserving the intimacy of the marital relationship. Hebrews 13:4 emphasizes the honor due to the marriage bed: "Marriage should be honored by all, and the marriage bed kept pure, for God will judge the adulterer and all the sexually immoral." By prioritizing physical connection and addressing issues openly, couples can protect their relationship from erosion and foster a deeper, more fulfilling bond. In doing so, they align with God's vision for marriage, characterized by mutual respect, love, and a commitment to each other's well-being.

Dr. Carla Marie Manly rightfully explains in her blog that just as a consistent level of open and honest verbal communication is an important element of a healthy marriage, communicating about sexual issues is also vital. Sexual intimacy is an important form of communication within a relationship. No marriage can function well when the beauty of sexuality is used in a harmful, controlling manner. Not only does a couple's sexual relationship allow for a physical release, but the intimacy component of sexuality provides a critical bonding element. Sexual intimacy offers couples a time to be emotionally close and open. A couple's sexual relationship can provide a connective "safe haven" from the outside world. When functioning well, a couple's sexual relationship creates and reinforces feelings of deep love, commitment, and trust.[33]

EMBRACING AND EVOLVING BEYOND DISAPPOINTMENT

In life, disappointments are inevitable—whether in work, family, friendships, or relationships. Succumbing to disappointment and

---

33. Carla Marie Manly, "Sex Wars: When Sex Is a Weapon in Your Marriage," *drcarlamanly blog*, October 25, 2018, Accessed April 3, 2024, https://www.drcarlamanly.com/sex-wars-when-sex-is-a-weapon-in-your-marriage/.

giving up only perpetuates a cycle of defeat. Those who persevere ultimately triumph, while those who quit never achieve success. This principle holds true across all aspects of life, including marriage. When facing disappointment in your spouse, it's important to consider not ending the relationship immediately. Every individual has imperfections; it's a consequence of our flawed nature due to sin.

Understanding that no one is perfect is indispensable to maintaining a healthy marital bond. In the complementary union of marriage, encountering disappointment is unavoidable. Both partners benefit from learning how to navigate these challenges through proactive communication and self-awareness. Remaining steadfast in your commitment to your marriage and honoring your vows is crucial.

Neil Anderson and Charles Mylander caution that disappointment calls for us to purify our spirits. We must remove the barriers to God's grace, truth, love, power, and righteousness. Our wrong reactions and self-protective behavior must go. Disappointment calls for our forgiveness…Disappointment calls for reevaluation…Disappointment calls for loving confrontation…The biggest disappointments of marriage sometimes hide the finest benefits. Turbulence leads to transition. Out of the worst often comes the best.[34]

Our love and care for our spouse should not hinge solely on their external actions. True love, rooted in godliness and authenticity, is unconditional and independent of external circumstances. It's the kind of love we should purposefully cultivate for our spouse, a choice we make to nurture and deepen our affection for them. As Gary Chapman asserts, "Love is not an emotion that comes over us or an elusive goal dependent on the actions of others. Authentic love

---

34. Anderson and Mylander, *The Christ-Centered Marriage*, 92.

is something within our capabilities, originating in our attitudes and culminating in our actions. If we think of it as a feeling, we shall be frustrated when we can't always work up that feeling. When we realize love is primarily an action, we are ready to use the tools we have to love better."[35]

UNCONDITIONAL LOVE:
THE ART OF SELFLESS CARING

Loving involves selflessly caring for one's spouse, a commitment that requires the elimination of selfishness. In marriage, selfishness is a significant obstacle to genuinely loving and pleasing your partner. The Bible emphasizes that love is not about personal gratification but about serving and valuing the other. Philippians 2:3-4 instructs, "Do nothing out of selfish ambition or vain conceit. Rather, in humility value others above yourselves, not looking to your own interests but each of you to the interests of the others." This passage highlights that genuine love requires setting aside personal desires to focus on the needs and well-being of one's spouse.

Janet Sadiku confirms how selfishness destroys relationships in these terms,

> Selfishness is the number one enemy of marriage. It threatens oneness/unity in marriage. Marriage cannot thrive or achieve much with selfish partners. Selfishness makes it difficult to compromise. It can lead to conflict, strife, infidelity, breaking marriage vow, separation, and divorce. It causes an inability to maintain a healthy, loving

---

35. Chapman, *Love as a Way of Life*, 6.

relationship. A selfish person goes from one divorce to another.[36]

Selfishness can profoundly disrupt marital harmony and lead to conflict. When each partner prioritizes their own needs and preferences over those of their spouse, it fosters an environment of resentment and discord. James 3:16 warns, "For where you have envy and selfish ambition, there you find disorder and every evil practice." This verse stresses that selfish ambitions create chaos and hinder the growth of a loving, supportive relationship. Couples who focus on their own interests rather than their partner's needs often find their marriage strained and their connection weakened.

Addressing selfishness in marriage involves embracing accountability and responsibility. Each spouse has specific roles and duties that contribute to the health of the marriage and household. Ephesians 5:33 states, "However, each one of you also must love his wife as he loves himself, and the wife must respect her husband." This verse emphasizes the importance of mutual love and respect, as well as clear roles and responsibilities. For example, if both partners agree to avoid certain behaviors or situations, they must adhere to these agreements to demonstrate commitment and respect.

The importance of mutual accountability extends to every aspect of marriage. Inconsistent adherence to agreed-upon principles or behaviors can undermine trust and create friction. Consistency in upholding responsibilities and respecting boundaries strengthens the marital bond and fosters trust. Proverbs 27:17 notes, "As iron sharpens iron,

---

36. Janet O. Sadiku et al., "Selfishness Breaks All the Ten Commandments," *International Journal of Trend in Scientific Research and Development* 7, no.1, (2023), https://www.ijtsrd.com/papers/ijtsrd52649.pdf.

so one person sharpens another." This principle highlights the need for both partners to support and hold each other accountable, refining their relationship through mutual effort and integrity.

Marriage requires continuous effort and mutual support to maintain its focus and purpose. Ecclesiastes 4:9 states, "Two are better than one because they have a good return for their labor." This verse illustrates the necessity of working together towards shared goals and mutual growth. Selfishness disrupts this cooperative effort, leading to marital strain. Couples must remain dedicated to their shared values and goals, addressing issues with humility and commitment to each other's well-being.

Selflessness and accountability are the cornerstones of a loving and fulfilling marriage. By prioritizing each other's needs, embracing defined roles, and working collaboratively towards common goals, couples uphold the sanctity and strength of their relationship. Marriage, as designed by God, flourishes when both partners are committed to loving each other unconditionally and maintaining mutual respect and responsibility. Couples can navigate challenges and build a resilient, deeply fulfilling partnership through such dedication.

DON'T BLAME YOUR SPOUSE
FOR YOUR UNHAPPINESS

It's crucial to avoid attributing your unhappiness to your spouse. Depending on your partner as the sole source of your happiness can create unrealistic expectations and strain your relationship. Blaming your spouse for your unhappiness is both unfair and counterproductive. The Bible teaches us that personal contentment and joy should come from our relationship with God rather than from others.

Philippians 4:11-13 reveals this truth: "I am not saying this because

I am in need, for I have learned to be content whatever the circumstances. I know what it is to be in need, and I know what it is to have plenty. I have learned the secret of being content in any and every situation, whether well-fed or hungry, whether living in plenty or in want. I can do all this through Him who gives me strength." Our fulfillment must ultimately come from God, not from our spouse.

Instead of focusing on receiving happiness from your spouse, strive to give and serve. This approach aligns with the biblical call to love and selflessness. Love is an active choice that involves giving and serving rather than seeking personal gain. By shifting the focus from what you can receive to what you can contribute, you align with God's design for relationships and foster a more nurturing and supportive marriage. The joy of serving in marriage brings a sense of fulfillment and contentment.

Dependence on God rather than on people for our sense of security and happiness is crucial. Psalm 46:1 declares, "God is our refuge and strength, an ever-present help in trouble." Placing your trust in God provides a wellspring of strength and peace that does not fluctuate with human fallibility. When God is your primary source of support and joy, you are less likely to be disappointed by the limitations of others. Your relationship with your spouse can then flourish, grounded in mutual respect and unconditional love.

Trusting in God enhances your ability to give and serve others, including your spouse. Proverbs 3:5-6 encourages, "Trust in the LORD with all your heart and lean not on your own understanding; in all your ways submit to Him, and He will make your paths straight." When you rely on God for inner security and strength, you are more equipped to offer genuine support and love to your partner. This trust empowers you, transforming your interactions into expressions of grace and kindness, enriching your marriage and drawing you closer together. As Jimmy Evans alerts, "Positive results occur when one trusts in God more than people or things. A person receives inner security and strength from He, who is faithful and who has unlimited resources. One can give more because giving flows from an internal resource. A person's life is filled with blessing, satisfaction, and optimism. One's realistic expectations of others draw one closer to them."[37]

Avoiding the blame game and focusing on God as your primary source of happiness is vital for a healthy marriage. You build a more resilient and loving relationship by cultivating a spirit of giving, relying on God's strength and trusting in His provision. Marriage thrives when both partners are committed to serving each other and finding their fulfillment in God rather than in the imperfections of human relationships. This approach leads to a deeper, more satisfying partnership that honors God's intentions for marriage. It also makes you feel responsible and accountable for your actions in the relationship.

·LOVE MANIFESTATION IN DIFFERENT STYLES

Love manifests in various forms. What type of love relationship do you aim to cultivate with your spouse, and what purpose does it serve within your marriage? Recognizing the significance, expressions, and impact of love on your personal and marital well-being is crucial for the overall health of your relationship. Understanding your love styles aids in conflict resolution, comprehension of your spouse, and assessing the level of happiness, contentment, and fulfillment in your romantic partnership.

---

37. Jimmy Evans, *Marriage on the Rock* (Dallas: XO Publishing, 2012), 9.

Love manifests in various forms, and understanding the types of love you and your spouse seek to cultivate is crucial for a healthy marriage. Different expressions of love impact your relationship in distinct ways, shaping how you connect and resolve conflicts. The Bible explains the importance of love in marriage and provides guidance on how it should be expressed. In 1 Corinthians 13:4-7, the Apostle Paul describes love as patient, kind, and devoid of selfishness or pride. Recognizing these characteristics helps you evaluate the health of your marital bond and ensure that your love aligns with biblical principles.

Understanding the different love styles can help you navigate your relationship more effectively. Love can be passionate and romantic, as seen in Eros; playful and fun, as in Ludus; or deep and enduring, as in Storge. Additionally, combinations of these styles, such as Mania (obsessive love), Pragma (practical love), and Agape (selfless love), can influence how you and your spouse interact. Each style brings unique dynamics into the relationship, impacting communication, conflict resolution, and overall satisfaction.

To maintain a strong marriage, it's necessary to pay attention to the "little things"—the daily acts of kindness and consideration that enhance your relationship. Proverbs 15:1 notes, "A gentle answer turns away wrath, but a harsh word stirs up anger." This principle highlights the importance of positive communication and the impact of small gestures on marital harmony. Criticism, when destructive, can harm the relationship, whereas a loving rebuke, aimed at constructive solutions, helps to address issues without damaging trust.

Avoiding familiarity and taking each other for granted are significant risks in marriage. The Bible encourages husbands and wives to continually nurture their relationship with affection and spontaneity. In Song of Solomon 2:10-13, we see a picture of romantic and spontaneous love, illustrating how this keeps the relationship vibrant and engaging. Regular expressions of love and appreciation, such as surprise date nights, love notes, or simple acts of service, help maintain the romance and courtship even after years of marriage, ensuring the bond remains strong and fulfilling.

God designed marriage to be a deep, intimate bond characterized by companionship, love, and mutual support. Genesis 2:24 highlights that marriage is a union between a man and a woman, meant to provide warmth, unity, and comfort. Cultivating a selfless attitude and placing your spouse's needs above your own desires promotes a stable and enriching relationship. As you work together, sharing goals and commitments, you strengthen your union and navigate challenges with resilience. Commitment is key to enduring and thriving in marriage and reflects the biblical call to love and support each other through all circumstances.

Marriage provides a profound and intimate bond. God's purpose in crafting marital unions is for partners to share companionship, love, encouragement, communication, warmth, unity, and comfort. Initially, God established marriage as a union between a biological man and a biological woman. Nurturing a selfless attitude towards our spouse cultivates a stable and enriching marital relationship, placing their needs above our own desires. This mindset promotes a wholesome and satisfying bond. As Gottman declares, "Not only will you increase the intimacy of your marriage by sharing your deepest goals with your spouse, but to the extent that you work together to achieve shared goals, they can be a path toward making your union even richer."[38]

---

38. John M. Gottman and Nan Silver, *Seven Principles for Making Marriage Work* (New York: Crown Publishers, Inc., 2021), 256.

CHAPTER III

CULTIVATING MARRIAGE HARMONY

I n exploring the application of godly marriage principles, it is important to ground our understanding in the truths of Scripture. A biblically faithful marriage reflects the divine design for relationships, rooted in the wisdom of Jesus Christ and the wisdom found in the Bible. According to Bible values, marriage is a sacred covenant between a man and a woman, established by God to mirror His relationship with His people.

This union is marked by mutual love, grace, patience, respect, forgiveness, commitment, understanding, and self-sacrifice. The husband is called to lead with Christ-like love, and the wife is invited to support and honor her husband. It also includes more values we will explore together in this chapter. Couples can cultivate a marriage that honors God and fosters deep, lasting joy and fulfillment by adhering to these principles. When we follow God's teachings, we thrive in our marriages. However, we suffer profound disappointment if we put God's decrees aside. Our modern world thinks it knows better than

God; however, the Bible says that the world's wisdom is foolishness to God (1 Corinthians 3:10).

CENTERING YOUR MARRIAGE IN GOD

The top principle of a stable and fulfilling marriage is making God the center of your household. For marital partners, this means prioritizing a godly approach in every aspect of their relationship. It requires embracing a love that mirrors God's unconditional love for humanity and integrating biblical values into the very fabric of the marital union. This commitment involves following Jesus Christ's teachings as a model and placing the Bible at the core of daily life, ensuring that all decisions and actions align with God's principles rather than personal desires or cultural norms.

Central to this godly approach is seeking God's guidance when faced with marital challenges. Instead of relying solely on human wisdom, couples should turn to prayer and Scripture. Establishing prayer as a daily practice, engaging in joint reading of the Bible, and making these spiritual activities a regular part of life help couples build a strong, faith-centered relationship. This approach ensures that the marital foundation is solid and unshakable, resting on the unchanging truths of God's Word rather than fluctuating personal opinions or societal pressures.

In any healthy relationship, God's role is foundational and multifaceted. He serves as a source of inspiration, a guiding force, and a standard for decisions and actions. Couples are encouraged to make their marital decisions in light of God's teachings without deviating from this sacred framework. This commitment to God as the center of their marriage fosters a relationship marked by joy, stability, and enduring love. By aligning their lives with God's principles, couples can experience a deeper partnership.

The importance of prioritizing God in marriage is evident in how it influences every aspect of married life. Couples who anchor their relationship in Jesus's principles often find greater peace, unity, and joy. Engaging in practices such as prayer, mutual reflection on Scripture, and maintaining a selfless attitude are required for nurturing a marriage that honors God. These practices are beneficial and vital for a thriving marital relationship that remains steadfast through life's circumstances.

Attempting to manage a marriage based solely on human wisdom and desires often leads to dissatisfaction and instability. The Bible consistently teaches that true marital success comes from aligning with God's standards rather than relying on one's own strength. Couples must recognize that God's power is necessary to achieve the kind of relationship He intends, and without His guidance, the effort to live by His principles can fall short.

Ultimately, a marriage centered on God reflects His love and purpose, creating a union characterized by mutual respect, commitment, and joy. By living out these biblical values and allowing God to guide their journey, couples can build a marriage that not only endures but thrives, manifesting the deep, lasting joy from a relationship anchored in divine truth.

Bill and Pam Farrell advise couples to establish fulfilling marriages by living spiritually. They insist that the more spiritual your marriage is, the more likely it is to be successful and sexually satisfying. The more passion you have toward God, the more you'll have available for your marriage. Do you see why Satan wants to keep you from praying, from reading the Bible, from getting to church? He knows those things will make a change for the better in your relationship. So, if spirituality is the most powerful tool in building a long-term, happy, and sexually satisfying relationship, how does a couple go about building their spiritual life? Decide to. That's plain and simple. Decide that spiritual life is just as important as being at the kids' soccer games.[39]

Prioritizing God in both individual lives and marital unions is indispensable in the quest to forge marriages that radiate godliness. It's the backbone upon which healthy and fulfilling marriages are built. It's important to anchor every aspect of married life in God's principles, emphasizing prayer, deep reflection on His teachings, and a selfless disposition as non-negotiable practices. For a marriage to thrive, God must be at its very core, breathing life into every interaction and decision.

FOSTERING RESPECT AND LOVE

Love and respect are inseparable companions and necessary components the Lord provides to strengthen our marriages. Without these foundational elements, no marriage can endure the trials and tribulations of life. In the divine design, a husband deeply desires and craves his wife's respect; and, while both partners indeed need respect, it is particularly crucial for men. God fashioned men to be leaders, and their need for respect is inherently tied to this role. In this context, respect means accepting and supporting their role as decision-makers, not belittling or undermining their authority. It involves allowing them to lead without unnecessary interference or unwarranted criticism, which enables them to thrive in their God-given responsibilities.

Men are wired to seek validation and feel appreciated when leading, protecting, and providing for their families. When a wife shows respect by valuing her husband's opinions and deferring to his leadership, she

---

39. Bill and Pam Farrell, *The Ten Best Decisions a Couple Can Make* (Eugene, OR: Harvest House Publishers, 2005), 176.

reinforces his role and strengthens his sense of purpose. This respect is not just a matter of outward actions but a reflection of genuine acknowledgment of his efforts and sacrifices.

When women express their respect through support and appreciation, men are more likely to be engaged, proactive, and fulfilled in their roles as husbands, fathers, and spiritual leaders. Conversely, when respect is absent, men can become passive and withdrawn, struggling to function fully as they feel diminished and emasculated. This dynamic is particularly evident in Western cultures, where cultural shifts have often reversed traditional roles, leading to confusion and dissatisfaction in many marriages.

Conversely, love is the core of a woman's emotional well-being in marriage. Women thrive on admiration, attention, and care from their husbands. They need to feel valued, safe, and protected. Affection is not just a "nice-to-have" but a critical aspect of loving a woman. Without consistent affection, a woman's emotional vitality can wither like a tree deprived of water. Just as men need respect to feel alive and valued, women need love to sustain their emotional health and connection with their husbands. A husband's affection and attention foster an environment where a wife feels cherished and cared for, leading to more harmony and fulfillment.

The principles of love and respect outlined in Scripture are not matters of personal preference or cultural opinion but divine truths established by God himself. Ignoring these principles can lead to broken marriages and lingering resentment. Activists may view these teachings as antiquated or restrictive, but those who adhere to these biblical principles often find themselves in stronger, more resilient marriages.

The Bible's teachings are not about enforcing rigid roles but about recognizing and nurturing the unique needs of each spouse as designed by our Creator. Honoring these principles leads to a thriving marriage, while disregarding them can result in conflict and separation. Ultimately, embracing God's design for love and respect is the key to a prosperous and lasting marriage. This insight is one of the most significant revelations bestowed by God to couples for constructing enduring and God-centered marriages. Neil Anderson contends that the most common pattern that surfaces in marital tension is loss of respect.[40]

Failure to appreciate, honor, and respect your spouse will likely result in your children lacking respect for your spouse. Consequently, they may struggle to respect their own spouses in their future marriages. As a parent, it's your responsibility to instill fundamental values of marriage in your children. Put differently, if you don't model respectful communication with your spouse, understand your role and responsibilities as a husband or wife, speak positively about your spouse to your children and shield them from negativity; your children may adopt this attitude towards marriage as the norm.

Moreover, your own marriage may suffer as a result. Satan opposes the success of every marriage. Through his deceit, modern society often discourages loving a disrespectful wife or respecting an unkind husband. Jesus did not sacrifice himself for us because we deserved love; instead, He did so out of unconditional love. In the same way, God calls us to love our spouses regardless of their faults, promising rewards both in this life and in the hereafter.

LOVING IN WORDS AND ACTIONS

Deciphering your spouse's love language is fundamental for deepening communication and creating a productive and fulfilling relationship.

---

40. Anderson and Mylander, *The Christ-Centered Marriage*, 102.

Simply expressing affection or intentions is not enough; effective communication of love requires learning and speaking your partner's specific love language. As D. Gary Chapman says, being sincere is not enough. We must be willing to learn our spouse's primary love language if we are to be effective communicators of love.[41] He added that the five love languages are words of affirmation, quality time, receiving gifts, acts of service, and physical touch.[42] To truly connect with your spouse, it is crucial to identify which resonates most deeply with them and incorporate it into your interactions.

For some people, receiving gifts is a primary love language. These gifts can range from small, meaningful tokens to more substantial presents. What matters most to them is the thoughtfulness and intentionality behind the gesture. They often value the element of surprise and the care involved in choosing a gift, so understanding which types of gifts resonate with your partner and making gift-giving a regular part of your relationship can create a memorable and cherished tradition.

Some individuals in this category also place significant value on material possessions as a source of fulfillment and joy, not as a weakness, but as a crucial part of their happiness. If you have such a partner and have different values, you might initially see them as materialistic or self-centered. However, recognizing that they appreciate gifts, regardless of their size or cost, can help you connect more deeply with them.

Conversely, some people's love language is deeply rooted in words of affirmation. They thrive on verbal validation and encouragement. For these individuals, expressing appreciation and affirmation in a

---

41. D. Gary Chapman, *The Five Love Languages: How to Express Heartfelt Commitment to Your Mate* (Chicago: Northfield Publishing, 1999), 15.

42. Ibid., 38.

tender, intimate, and caring way is crucial. It's not about being insincere but communicating affection through supportive and loving words.

The key is to ensure your verbal expressions match their need for validation and emotional support. For these partners, a lack of verbal appreciation or recognition of their efforts to please you or care for the household can cause significant emotional hurt. Their sense of worth and self-esteem are closely tied to your recognition and verbal affirmations. They flourish when you affirm and appreciate them with your words.

Another love language for others is acts of service, in which affection is expressed through helpful actions rather than words. This can involve tasks such as cooking a meal, assisting with household chores, or running errands. Actions often speak louder than words for those who value this love language. They find practical support, whether helping with daily responsibilities, supporting them through work or personal challenges, or caring for a family member, to be deeply meaningful.

For these individuals, verbal expressions of love, care, and appreciation are less significant than tangible actions. They measure love by what you do rather than what you say. Without concrete and practical expressions of love, your words might not resonate with them as much as you might expect. If your spouse values acts of service, they may feel disappointed or even resentful if you rely solely on verbal affirmations. They thrive on actions that demonstrate love and care.

Physical touch is another love language and centers on physical intimacy and closeness. For those who value this language, gestures such as cuddling, kissing, hugging, holding hands, and enjoying close contact are important to feeling loved and connected. These physical expressions are fundamental to their emotional well-being. In their world, the absence of such affection makes them feel neglected or undervalued.

To nurture a strong emotional bond, it's vital to weave physical affection into your everyday interactions. Even if you're not naturally inclined towards physical touch, making an effort to incorporate it into your routine is crucial. Your spouse deeply needs and yearns for your physical presence, so it's important not to overlook this aspect of your relationship. While it's understandable that some people may feel uncomfortable with physical touch, especially if it's not their primary love language, it's wise to recognize and respect your spouse's needs.

Marriage involves balancing your own comfort with the effort to meet your partner's emotional needs. Even if physical touch doesn't come naturally to you, consciously engaging in it can significantly strengthen your relationship. It's about extending beyond your own preferences to ensure your partner feels valued and cherished. Ultimately, marriage isn't just about pleasing yourself but about finding joy in making your partner happy. Understanding and embracing their love language, even when it challenges your comfort zone, is a testament to your commitment and love.

Quality time is another important love language centered on undivided attention and shared experiences. Those who value this language cherish moments when their complete focus is dedicated to their partner, whether engaging in deep conversations, playing games, or embarking on outings and vacations. Discovering what specific types of quality time resonate most with your spouse is vital. What constitutes quality time can vary significantly from one person to another, so it's crucial to understand your spouse's unique preferences rather than applying a one-size-fits-all approach.

Quality time isn't always achievable daily, but when you set aside time, your spouse desires your full presence without distractions from phones, kids, friends, or work. They seek productive, meaningful, and memorable moments, creating lasting impressions and genuine joy. These moments might involve varying levels of monetary investment, but their actual value lies in the depth of connection and enjoyment you share.

Regardless of your primary love language, making time for quality moments is beneficial for every marriage. It's about keeping the relationship vibrant and alive, ensuring both partners feel valued and engaged. Investing in quality time strengthens your bond and enriches the overall experience of being together. Every marriage benefits from finding and prioritizing these special moments, keeping the connection fresh and exciting.

To instill or reignite a sense of commitment to marriage, we must deliberately express our love to our spouse through both verbal and non-verbal means. You almost always go right expressing your love to your spouse in their love language. Regardless of the dire state of your marriage or the severity of the circumstances, unconditional love can transform your spouse's heart; but it must begin with your own.

You can build a harmonious and deeply satisfying relationship by genuinely learning and implementing your partner's preferred expressions of love and respect and fulfilling the mutual responsibilities of love and respect. Our efforts to show love are often not reciprocated or appreciated because they do not align with our partner's love language. This misalignment can result in resentment and dissatisfaction. By learning and applying your spouse's love language, you can express your love more meaningfully and valuably, fostering a more positive and satisfying relationship. In essence, expressing love in a way that resonates with your spouse leads to a happier and more fulfilling partnership. This approach ensures that love is communicated effectively and continuously, fostering a robust and enduring bond.

EMBRACE GRACE AND FORGIVENESS

In any marriage, consistently prioritizing forgiveness and grace is important for fostering a healthy and enduring relationship. Grace is the act of showing kindness and mercy to someone who doesn't deserve it, just as God has shown us grace through Christ. Forgiveness, on the other hand, is the act of pardoning an offense or mistake. A lack of these virtues significantly contributes to today's elevated divorce rates.

Regardless of their secular or religious beliefs, people often struggle with holding onto resentments, even within church communities. The Bible highlights forgiveness and grace as foundational elements of lasting relationships. Despite the tendency of popular media to glorify retaliation, the biblical perspective emphasizes forgiveness and love as central principles that should guide our interactions with others.

Biblical teachings outline the crucial role of forgiveness in nurturing a lasting marriage. Mirroring the grace that Christ extends to us, forgiveness involves extending grace to a partner even when they may not seem to deserve it. This concept shows that forgiveness is not contingent on the other person's worthiness but is an act of grace reflecting Christ's unconditional love. The essence of true forgiveness lies in giving grace freely, without expecting anything in return, and acknowledging that no transgression is too great to be forgiven.

Empathy and forgiveness are often scarce in contemporary relationships, yet they are vital for a strong and resilient marriage. The understanding that believers did not earn forgiveness from God helps clarify why we should extend it to others. Forgiveness is a divine gift rather than a response to merit, emphasizing that extending grace to a partner, regardless of their actions, is a fundamental aspect of a loving relationship. Ruth Bell Graham, wife to evangelist Billy Graham, is known for this saying, "A happy marriage is the union of two good forgivers,"[43] embodying a commitment to grace and understanding.

Scriptural guidance provides practical advice for enhancing marital relationships. James 5:16 encourages individuals to confess their shortcomings and pray for one another, promoting mutual healing and strengthening the marital bond. Similarly, Proverbs 15:1 teaches that a gentle response can defuse anger and prevent conflict. Practicing kindness and gentleness in daily interactions is crucial for maintaining harmony within the marriage. These virtues create an environment where both partners can grow and support each other and foster a nurturing and loving relationship.

By adhering to God's values and principles, couples can uphold the sanctity of marriage and counteract negative influences. This commitment involves practicing forgiveness, extending grace, and showing kindness in everyday interactions. In doing so, couples honor God through their relationship, reflecting His love and grace. Upholding these virtues strengthens the marital bond and fosters a relationship that not only endures but flourishes in the face of challenges.

As Markman et al. concisely declare, if you've been wronged by your partner, it's up to you to forgive or not. Your partner can't do this for you. It's your choice. If you've wronged your partner in some way, it's your job to take responsibility for your actions. You need to apologize and mean it. Further, if needed, take steps to see that whatever you did doesn't happen again. This assumes that the infraction

---

43. Ruth Bell Graham, *It's My Turn* (Grand Rapids, MI: Zondervan, 1980), 52.

is clear and that you are both humble and mature enough to take responsibility.[44]

BIBLICAL VIEW ON DIVORCE

Believers should understand divorce in the light of the Word of God, not according to cultural norms. Moses, Jesus, and Paul addressed divorce from the Old to the New Testament perspectives. In the Old Testament, specifically in Deuteronomy 24:1-4, Moses provides regulations concerning divorce. He allows for divorce in cases where a husband finds "some indecency" in his wife. However, the exact meaning of "indecency" has been interpreted differently over time. In its original context, it was understood as a broad category that could encompass various forms of serious moral or sexual misconduct that disrupted the marital covenant. The term was intended to protect the dignity and rights of women by ensuring that divorce could only be pursued if a significant breach of trust or integrity occurred.

Over time, interpretations have ranged from viewing "indecency" as any form of sexual immorality to more narrowly defining it as a severe and specific violation of the marriage bond. In the New Testament, particularly Jesus's teachings (Matthew 19:3-9) and Paul's (1 Corinthians 7:10-15) further refine the understanding of divorce, emphasizing that while it is permitted in cases of marital unfaithfulness or abandonment, it should not be approached lightly.

Thus, while Moses's regulations provided a legal framework for divorce, Jesus and Paul called believers to a higher standard, emphasizing reconciliation and forgiveness wherever possible. Understanding

---

44. Howard J. Markman, Scott M. Stanley, and Susan L. Blumberg, *Fighting for Your Marriage*, 3rd ed. (San Francisco: Jossey-Bass, 2010), 353.

"indecency" in light of the broader biblical narrative helps believers navigate the complexities of marriage and divorce with wisdom and grace, staying true to the principles in Scripture.

In the New Testament, Jesus discussed divorce in several passages, including Matthew 5:31-32 and Matthew 19:3-9. Jesus emphasizes the sacredness and permanence of marriage, stating that Moses permitted divorce due to the hardness of people's hearts but that it was not part of God's original plan for marriage. He teaches that divorce, except for cases of sexual immorality (*porneia*), leads to adultery if either partner remarries. Jesus's teachings on divorce set a high standard for marital fidelity and commitment,

In his letters, particularly in 1 Corinthians 7, Paul provides guidance on marriage and divorce within the context of the early Christian community. Paul acknowledges the challenges believers face in mixed marriages (where one partner believes in Christ and the other does not). He advises them to remain married if possible, as the unbelieving spouse may be sanctified through the believing spouse.

However, he also acknowledges that in cases of an unbelieving spouse who chooses to leave, the believer is not bound in such circumstances. While Moses provides regulations for divorce in the Old Testament, Jesus presents a more stringent view emphasizing the sanctity of marriage, and Paul offers practical advice for believers navigating marital challenges within the early Christian community.

Instone-Brewer succinctly summarizes the legitimate grounds for divorce, "The Old Testament recognizes four grounds for divorce. The first three are neglecting to provide food, clothing, and conjugal love (by either husband or wife), and the fourth is committing adultery in which "the only person who would enact a divorce was the victim."[45] He adds:

> Jesus says that divorce should never happen because when two people marry, they are joined by God, who is a witness to the marriage vows and is there to bless the marriage. These vows should never be broken—especially since they are made before God…Jesus never says that these vows are impossible to break—as if God ignores the reality of sin—but he teaches that if a partner breaks the vows and is then repentant, we should forgive that person. If the vows are continuously broken without repentance, then the marriage will be left in shreds. Therefore, although the breakup of a marriage is always due to sin, it is not the divorce itself that is the sin; the sin is the breaking of the vows, which causes the divorce.[46]

According to a recent national survey, people in the US divorce for several reasons, including lack of commitment, the most common reason given by divorcing couples (73%). Other reasons are frequent arguments (56%), infidelity (55%), unrealistic expectations (45%), lack of marriage preparation (41%), and domestic violence (25%).[47]

When confronted with serious issues such as infidelity, domestic violence, cruelty, or abuse in a marriage, it's important to recognize that these challenges can deeply damage the relationship. Much like

---

45. David Instone-Brewer, *Divorce and Remarriage in the Church: Biblical Solutions for Pastoral Realities* (Downers Grove: IVP Books, 2001), 36-37.

46. Ibid., 18.

47. Gitnux, "The Main Reasons for Divorce Statistics 2023," *GITNUXBLOG*, Last modified March 20, 2023, Accessed May 13, 2023, https://blog.gitnux.com/reasons-for-divorce-statistics/.

untreated cancer, these problems can eventually lead to the end of the marriage if not addressed promptly. This analogy highlights the critical need for timely intervention and healing to prevent irreparable harm.

A Christian might consider alternative approaches when a marriage reaches such a critical state. One alternative is to seek professional counseling or therapy to help with the underlying issues and work toward reconciliation. Another possibility is to engage in a structured separation with clear goals and timelines, allowing both partners time to reflect and grow and not divorce.

Additionally, some might consider seeking support from a faith community to help mediate and provide guidance through the conflict. The final alternative is simply divorce. Each of these solutions involves a thoughtful balance of faith, practical steps, and mutual effort to address and resolve the marital issues. Remember to use God's Word and insight first and last. By exploring these different avenues, individuals facing a troubled marriage can find a path that aligns with their values and offers the best chance for resolution, whether that means restoring the relationship or preparing for a different future.

WHY THE BIBLE DISAPPROVES OF COHABITATION

Cohabitation, or the practice of living together in a romantic relationship without formal marriage, has increasingly gained popularity across the globe. This trend is evident in both non-Western and Western countries, reflecting a shift in societal attitudes toward traditional institutions and relationships. Historically, cohabitation has emerged as a response to changing norms about marriage, often driven by a desire for greater personal freedom, economic considerations, or evolving cultural values.

From a biblical perspective, cohabitation is viewed as intrinsically immoral because it fundamentally undermines the commitment and sanctity of marriage. The Bible emphasizes that sexual relations are reserved for the bonds of marriage, as highlighted in Hebrews 13:4: "Marriage should be honored by all, and the marriage bed kept pure, for God will judge the adulterer and all the sexually immoral." This scriptural principle deepens the belief that sexual intimacy is intended to be a sacred expression of a committed, lifelong covenant between a husband and wife.

Historically, traditional marriage has been upheld as a vital social institution designed to reflect commitment and provide a stable foundation for family life. Cohabitation, by contrast, is seen as a rejection of these foundational elements, potentially weakening the marriage commitment that the Bible upholds. In a global context, while cultural practices and attitudes may vary, the biblical teaching remains clear: adherence to God's design for marriage is essential for maintaining the purity and integrity of the marital relationship.

EMBRACE PERSONAL CHANGE
AND FOSTER GROWTH
THROUGH AFFIRMATION

True transformation begins with "self." If you wish for change in your relationship or desire change in your spouse, you must first examine and address your own actions and attitudes. Expecting others to alter their behavior while remaining unchanged is unrealistic. Personal change, though challenging, is the foundational step toward a successful and evolving relationship. In marriage, certain fundamental issues, such as infidelity, substance abuse, irresponsible behavior, and emotional neglect, are non-negotiable. However, beyond these deal-breakers, there is always room for improvement in every individual, and acknowledging this is key to nurturing a healthier relationship.

Personal growth requires deep and sincere introspection. This involves thoroughly examining your actions, words, and attitudes and a reflective appreciation of your journey. When this process is integrated into the context of a marital relationship, it becomes a pathway to personal development and enhancing the connection with your spouse. A mindset of gratitude and appreciation is recommended. Recognizing the good in yourself and your spouse can significantly contribute to the growth and strengthening of your relationship.

Affirmation and appreciation play pivotal roles in encouraging positive change in your partner. By expressing gratitude and acknowledging the value of your spouse's efforts, you create an environment where they feel valued and motivated to improve. Even small efforts may go unappreciated without such recognition and cease over time. Everyone thrives on acknowledgment and positive reinforcement, whether in marriage, work, or other relationships. Thus, fostering a culture of appreciation within your relationship can lead to more meaningful and sustained growth.

The key to influencing positive change in your partner starts with changing yourself. It also involves recognizing and valuing the small things you may have overlooked. There is always something worthy of appreciation in your partner. If you try to observe and celebrate these aspects, it can inspire your partner to grow and contribute positively to the relationship. For instance, if your spouse is not inclined to engage in spiritual practices like reading the Bible or praying, you can set an example by practicing these activities yourself and sharing them with your spouse gently and neutrally.

Expressing gratitude towards your spouse and being thankful to the Lord for bringing them into your life is crucial. Never take the little things for granted. Showing appreciation for both the minor and significant aspects of your partner's contributions fosters a positive atmosphere. This approach motivates changes in attitude and behavior and cultivates a thriving and supportive relationship. As emphasized by Julie Clinton, "Gratitude and affirmation are the key ingredients in any relational change. Start there and work on your own heart and thoughts first."[48]

Personal transformation and relational growth are intertwined processes. By initiating change within yourself and expressing sincere appreciation to your spouse, you lay the groundwork for a more fulfilling and dynamic relationship. Such efforts lead to mutual growth and a deeper connection, ultimately enhancing the overall health of your marriage.

ROLES AND RESPONSIBILITIES

The distinction between traditional and contemporary gender roles has become increasingly ambiguous and contentious in modern discourse. This shift often leads to confusion and contradictions about the expectations and responsibilities within marriage. In navigating these complexities, couples must seek and adhere to the divine design for gender roles as outlined in Scripture. Understanding this divine framework can help create a harmonious, secure, and serene atmosphere within marriage.

Traditional gender roles, historically rooted in cultural and societal norms, often defined clear distinctions between male and female responsibilities. In contrast, contemporary perspectives

---

48. Julie Clinton, *Ten Things You Aren't Telling Him: How to Help the Man in Your Life Love You Better* (Eugene: Harvest House Publishers, 2009), 195.

frequently blur these lines, advocating for more fluid and egalitarian approaches to gender roles. This ambiguity can lead to misunderstandings and conflicts in marital relationships, where both partners may struggle to reconcile their expectations with their roles within the marriage.

Biblically, gender roles are grounded in the creation narrative and the teachings of the New Testament. Genesis 2:18 states that God created Eve as a complementary partner to Adam, highlighting the idea that men and women were designed to work together in a complementary manner. This design emphasizes that each spouse has distinct yet equally valuable roles.

Additionally, 1 Peter 3:1-7 reinforces these principles by emphasizing respectful and understanding behavior from both spouses. The Bible envisions a partnership where roles are not about dominance or inequality but about fulfilling God's design for harmonious living. The husband is called to lead with humility and love, while the wife is called to support and respect her husband, creating a balance that fosters a secure and nurturing environment.

Adhering to these biblical principles can help couples transcend the confusion and contradictions of modern gender role debates. Embracing the divine design for gender roles encourages a marriage characterized by mutual respect, love, and support. This approach aligns with God's intention for marriage, allowing couples to cultivate a relationship that reflects His wisdom and brings about a peaceful and stable home.

Let's dive deeper. God appointed man as the head of the household, entrusting him with significant responsibilities rather than mere authority. This role entails providing, protecting, and serving as the family's spiritual leader. It does not grant dominance over one's wife but calls for love, care, and protection. As God defines it, authentic leadership is rooted in service and sacrificial love, not in control or superiority. Yet, influenced by Satan, our contemporary society has devised methods to defy the divine laws and principles established for successful marriages.

In contemporary Western culture, the foundational roles within marriage have been upended. What was once clear and true has been reversed, and society now often accepts these distortions as the new moral norms. Yet, God's principles remain unchanged. He established these rules and roles, and His laws are eternal. While cultural norms evolve, God's truth remains constant. The confusion that we see today does not alter the divine order that God has set.

God's design for marriage, as outlined in Scripture, assigns specific roles. The divine arrangement of men as leaders and women as suitable helpers is not subject to personal preference or societal trends. The term "suitable helper" does not imply inferiority or servitude but rather a complementary role that supports and enhances the husband's leadership. Whether one finds it agreeable or not, this is the structure God established. We cannot selectively adhere to God's laws based on cultural shifts. Following Christ means adhering to God's intended design rather than conforming to cultural expectations.

In essence, by upholding the roles established by God, both husband and wife can experience a marriage that reflects divine order and purpose. It's about adhering to roles and inviting God's blessings and peace into the marriage. Embracing these roles leads to a harmonious and fulfilling relationship consistent with God's eternal wisdom.

Understanding and accepting God's design for marriage is crucial for experiencing the fullness of His blessings. The roles He has established are not arbitrary but meant to enhance and enrich the marital relationship. By respecting and honoring these roles, both partners can enjoy a loving marriage aligned with God's will.

I understand that not all men naturally take on leadership roles, and some may shy away from the responsibilities that come with it. However, it's crucial to involve them in decision-making processes, even if they struggle with their own decisions, let alone those affecting the whole household. Despite these challenges, the principles laid out in God's order remain unchanged. It's clever to find ways to make the system work effectively and help them embrace their role in leadership without undermining their sense of worth or diminishing their role.

Dr. Tony Evans, in his Bible Study Book *Kingdom Man: Every Man's Destiny, Every Woman's Dream*, expresses that a kingdom man is a male who places himself under the rule of God and lives His life in submission to the lordship of Jesus Christ. Instead of following his own way, a kingdom man seeks to know God's will and to carry out God's kingdom agenda on earth. When a kingdom man functions according to the principles and precepts of the kingdom, there will be order and provision. When he doesn't, he opens himself and those around him to chaos.[49] As Vern Sheridan Poythress adds, "Just as husbands and fathers ought to exercise godly leadership in their human families, so wise, mature men ought to be appointed as fatherly leaders in the church (1 Timothy 3:1-7)."[50]

God also designated women as suitable helpers for men. This designation does not imply subordination to man but signifies compatibility, complementarity, and fulfillment. In essence, a man is incomplete

---

49. Evans, *Kingdom Man*, 19.

50. Vern Sheridan Poythress, *Recovering Biblical Manhood and Womanhood*, ed. John Piper and Wayne Grudem (Wheaton, IL: Crossway, 1991), 237-50.

without a woman by his side. The creation of woman was a necessary step to fulfill this purpose. It signifies that God desires women to contribute to shaping their husbands (and vice versa) into individuals who reflect the likeness of Christ, thus facilitating mutual transformation. As Smalley states, "God never created a woman to be a doormat. She is meant to be a vital life-giving part of the home." [51]

However, this does not imply that the woman assumes the role of head of the household, as is erroneously advocated and embraced by our modern society. Reversing roles, as the current cultural mindset encourages, is not biblical and leads to upheaval and disarray within the home. Challenging God's established order within the household is tantamount to challenging His authority as the Creator. Men must embrace full responsibility, overcome passivity and fear, and lead their families following biblical principles. They are to make decisions grounded in Scripture and fulfill their roles as leaders within the family, as God originally intended. Women serve as suitable helpers, and men are heads of the household.

To this end, Tony Evans contends that the problem keeping many men in our culture today from being kingdom men is that they have relinquished their God-given right to rule, either through silence or blame. Instead of loving the fact that they are men and therefore are responsible by nature, they flee from their responsibility. And they always seem to find a reason not to own up to what it means to be a man. As a result, men have given up their opportunity to approach the Christian life as a challenge to conquer and rule well. [52]

As the head of the household, a man should prioritize establishing

---

51. Gary T. Smalley, *For the Better or for the Best: A Valuable Guide to Knowing, Understanding, and Loving Your Husband* (Grand Rapids: Zondervan Publishing House, 1979), 22.

52. Evans, *Kingdom Man*, 26.

a solid relationship with his spouse and assume the role of their family's protector, provider, and spiritual guide. Together, they build their own family unit, minimizing direct and constant interference from external opinions and influences of their respective families and friends.

This entails spouses reducing their reliance on their families and friends financially, emotionally, and physically. They must learn to rely on each other independently, making autonomous decisions for their family and fostering mutual dependence unless circumstances necessitate otherwise, rather than out of mere preference. This encourages emotional, spiritual, financial, and mental intimacy and growth, thus fostering a nurturing environment where they can flourish as a couple and a family.

E. Dadang Mipo states that marriage means to leave and to cleave. "For this cause, a man shall leave his father and mother and cleave to his wife, and they shall become one flesh" (Genesis 2:24). It is interesting to note from this biblical text that the leaving of father and mother was strictly to the man and not specifically to the woman. In the biblical context, the man is the one to do the cleaving to his wife. I am of the opinion that the reason for this action is because, in God's point of view, the man is always the head.[53]

Roles and responsibilities in marriage involve adhering to God's divine prescribed guidance. Men are called to lead, and women are to be suitable helpers. This arrangement, though counter to contemporary cultural norms, is designed by God for the benefit of the family. Following these principles brings about deeper love and respect and

---

53. E. Dadang Mipo, "Social Relations and Implications on Families in Africa: Applying Biblical Principles of Marital Practices Amongst Contemporary Husbands and Wives Relationships," *Journal of African Interdisciplinary Studies* 6, no.6 (June2022): 91105, http://cedred.org/jais/ images/june2022/PDF_Mipo_Dadang_Social_Relations_and_Implications_on_Families_in_Africa.pdf.

aligns with God's unchanging truth. Embrace these roles to experience the true peace and joy that come from living according to God's design for marriage.

MARRIAGE IS A SACRED COVENANT

Marriage, as described in Scripture, is not merely a social contract or legal arrangement, but a sacred covenant established by God. This covenantal nature of marriage reflects the profound spiritual and relational significance that God intended from the beginning. When we marry, we become "one flesh" with our partner, as stated in Genesis 2:24: "For this reason, a man will leave his father and mother and be united to his wife, and they will become one flesh." This unity signifies more than physical closeness; it denotes a deep, intertwined bond where each partner is committed to the well-being and flourishing of the other. The concept of one flesh implies a deep emotional, spiritual, and physical connection, where the two partners are no longer individuals but a unified entity.

In Matthew 22:39, Jesus teaches us to "love your neighbor as yourself," a principle that should profoundly influence how we interact with our spouse. This command reinforces the importance of treating our partner with the same love, respect, and consideration that we desire for ourselves. It reinforces the idea that marriage is built on mutual care and selflessness, reflecting the nature of God's love for humanity.

Marriage as a covenant is sacred and unique, designed by God to be a pure and honorable relationship. It is not a mere arrangement to be altered based on convenience or personal preference but a solemn promise that mirrors God's commitment to His people. In Ephesians 5:31-32, Paul describes marriage as a profound mystery that illustrates the relationship between Christ and the Church. This analogy highlights that marriage is intended to be a living representation of the covenantal love and faithfulness that Christ has for His Church.

God instituted marriage to reflect His divine relationship with us, characterized by fidelity, commitment, and mutual respect. This divine purpose enhances the importance of preserving and honoring marriage according to God's original design. Any deviation from this purpose undermines the sacredness of the marital bond and diminishes its ability to reflect God's intentions.

Therefore, deep respect for marriage involves recognizing and upholding its sacred nature. Couples are called to cherish their union, honor their vows, and embody the love and commitment God exemplifies. By doing so, they honor the covenant they have entered into and reflect the divine relationship that marriage is meant to symbolize.

Michael and Kendra Holmes assert that the sacredness of marriage should be revered as a crucial expression of every spouse's life. Marriage isn't as simple as the uniting of two individuals through paper and law. It is a most holy covenant between each husband and wife and a covenant between that couple and the Lord. When done in the right spirit, every couple can have a God-fearing and God-favored married life. Marriage is sacred because its foundational truths are rooted in the Holy Word of God; He made it clear that marriage is meant to be holy and should be treated with the utmost respect. That's not an expired word. Time doesn't have the power or the permission to shift or alter what God says.[54]

---

54. Michael and Kendra Holmes, "The Importance of Sanctity of Marriage," *The Houston Home Journal*, March 22, 2023, Accessed April 21, 2024, https://hhjonline.com/the-importance-of-sanctity-of-marriage-p19276-191.htm.

CONTROLLING YOUR ANGER

While experiencing anger is inevitable, mastering its control is vital to safeguarding your marriage from ruin. Succumbing to unchecked anger can result in irreparable harm, with consequences that may prove impossible to rectify. The expression of anger can repulse a caring partner, causing emotional, mental, and physical distance to ensue. This transforms your home into an inhospitable atmosphere.

Your aspiration is for your marriage to cultivate a nurturing and inviting environment conducive to the well-being of you, your spouse, and your children. Refuse to allow anger to dictate the trajectory of your marriage. If anger is a recurring issue for you, prioritize learning effective anger management strategies. The Bible offers several principles for managing anger effectively:

Self-control: Proverbs 16:32 states, "Better a patient person than a warrior, one with self-control than one who takes a city." Cultivating self-control is indispensable in managing anger constructively.

Be Quick to Listen, Slow to Speak, Slow to Anger: James 1:19 advises, "My dear brothers and sisters, take note of this: Everyone should be quick to listen, slow to speak, and slow to become angry." Actively listening and carefully considering before responding can help prevent impulsive anger-fueled reactions.

Avoid Retaliation: Romans 12:17-21 encourages believers to overcome evil with good and leave vengeance to God. Responding to anger with kindness and forgiveness can defuse conflicts and promote reconciliation.

Seek Wise Counsel: Proverbs 15:22 advises seeking counsel from wise individuals to gain perspective and guidance in managing anger effectively.

Prayer and Reflection: Ephesians 4:26-27 encourages believers to address anger promptly but without sin and to not let anger linger unresolved. Praying for wisdom, patience, and peace in moments of anger helps foster emotional regulation and spiritual growth.

Forgiveness: Colossians 3:13 urges believers to forgive others as the Lord has forgiven them. Letting go of resentment and bitterness can release the hold of anger and promote emotional healing.

By incorporating these principles into their lives, married couples can cultivate healthier responses to anger and manage their emotions in accordance with biblical teachings.

GROWING PATIENCE AND GRACE

Growing patience and grace within a marriage is vital to maintaining a healthy and satisfactory relationship. God-given patience and grace are powerful tools for controlling anger and fostering understanding between partners. These qualities are not merely reactive but proactive virtues that help build a solid foundation of love and mutual respect.

Empathy is critical in this process. By developing empathy, we strive to genuinely understand our partner's perspective, which allows us to respond with compassion rather than frustration and disdain. Empathy helps us to see situations from our partner's point of view, acknowledging their feelings and experiences. This understanding can defuse anger and prevent conflicts from escalating, shifting our focus from personal grievances to a collective effort to address issues together.

When empathy is absent, it erects a barrier to emotional connection. Partners may feel misunderstood or invalidated, leading to emotional disconnection and dissatisfaction. This disconnection, if left unaddressed, can lead to deeper relational issues, including unfaithfulness and even divorce. A lack of empathy undermines the trust and intimacy vital for a strong marriage, making resolving conflicts and forgiving one another difficult.

Patience and grace, fueled by empathy, are the key to navigating the inevitable challenges of marriage with a spirit of forgiveness. Marriage involves joys and struggles, and it is natural for partners to hurt each other occasionally. However, when patience and grace are actively cultivated, they allow partners to handle these hurts with understanding rather than bitterness. This approach is crucial in preventing the growth of unforgiveness and supports healing and reconciliation.

By embracing patience and grace, couples can build a resilient relationship where disagreements are addressed with respect and love. Empathy helps partners stay connected and committed, fostering an environment where both individuals feel valued and heard. This relational dynamic promotes long-term harmony, strengthens the marital bond, and makes it possible to endure and overcome the challenges that arise along the journey of marriage.

PRAY FOR YOUR MARRIAGE, FAMILY, AND SPOUSE

In relationships, prayer is an indispensable pillar for sustaining and nurturing a healthy marriage. When faced with trials and tribulations, a marriage may be troubled without earnest and consistent prayer. Prayer is the foundation that fortifies and sustains a relationship against inevitable life challenges. The necessity of prayer cannot be overstated. We are engaged in a spiritual battle with an invisible adversary whose primary objective is to undermine and destroy our relationships. This enemy operates relentlessly, seeking to steal joy, peace, and harmony from our lives and even kill us.

Many believers, especially in Western contexts, remain unaware of the subtle yet profound impact of this spiritual adversary. They often attribute their struggles and frustrations to their spouses rather than recognizing the enemy's influence. While it is true that every person has character flaws, it is crucial to understand that the enemy can exploit these flaws to create discord. The adversary aims to divert our attention from the source of our struggles, making us focus on superficial issues rather than the underlying spiritual conflict. By understanding this, we can better navigate our marital challenges and address them with a clear perspective.

Your partner may indeed have attitudes or behaviors that need to be addressed; but ignoring them could harm your relationship. However, it's crucial to recognize that the real enemy often causes more turmoil than anything else. He'll distort your perception, making you see issues that aren't there and distracting you from lifting your partner in prayer, leading to unnecessary arguments. Recognizing the real enemy reassures us and guides our approach to marital challenges.

Remember: everything that happens on earth has its roots in the spiritual realm. Many of our conflicts originated from spiritual forces. Therefore, you must confront the real source of these issues through prayer and intercession. Don't engage in battles against the enemy of your union in the wrong way. Knowing your enemy is decisive for victory. Now that you understand who he is, fight him effectively.

The enemy thrives on our ignorance of his tactics. He operates in a stealth mode, making it easy to place blame on our partners instead of confronting the real issue. This misdirection often leads to prolonged conflict and dissatisfaction. Just as one would combat a physical illness by targeting the illness itself, we must fight the spiritual forces behind our marital difficulties. Recognizing and addressing the root cause is vital rather than merely dealing with its effects. Understanding the enemy's tactics prepares us for the battle ahead.

When Satan aims to undermine your relationship, he often presents misleading information. The truth is crucial; only God holds the whole and accurate truth. If there's any doubt, reflect on the account from the Garden of Eden. Satan deceived Eve with falsehoods that seemed plausible and appealing. He often employs tactics that appear truthful and attractive to lure believers away from God's revealed truth. This is why many Christians today fall prey to modern cultural norms and practices, mistaking them for the divine truth.

Similarly, Satan distorts information about your marriage. He exaggerates a minor issue to make you believe your marriage is failing or your spouse is the problem. Remember, God's blessings are meant to bring joy, peace, and fulfillment, not sorrow. It's important to remember that God brought you together and blessed your union. When doubts arise, they are often rooted in the enemy's lies rather than the reality of God's truth.

Devote time and effort to pray and intercede for your marriage. God has the power to turn things around and bring more incredible blessings than before. He is the God of miracles and can change any situation. Resist the temptation to succumb to hopelessness and despair, knowing God remains sovereign. Seek His guidance before making decisions about your marriage. In every action and choice, make sure you consult with God first. Pray diligently to your heavenly Father, in Jesus's name. The name that destroys strongholds, powers, dominions, authorities, demons, and dark forces behind our sufferings.

Satan consistently offers misleading information (lies). Be cautious, especially when it seems reassuring but feels wrong deep in your heart. Jesus said you will recognize the truth by its fruits and that the truth will set you free. True guidance from Jesus brings clarity, peace, and restoration, not guilt or confusion. Trust in the Lord's guidance and persist in prayer. He will lead your steps and decisions, providing your marriage with stability.

As spouses, it is our duty to fervently pray for our partners, our families, and our children. A spouse who diligently prays for their partner contributes significantly to a thriving marriage. Conversely, neglecting to pray can be detrimental to the marital bond. Prayer is never wasted; it is a powerful tool that unlocks and unleashes God's guidance, protection, and blessings on our lives.

When praying for your spouse, be specific. Pray for their physical health, emotional stability, spiritual growth, financial security, and professional success. Pray that the Lord blesses them with wisdom, aligns their character with the teachings of Jesus (becoming more like Jesus), and guides them in fulfilling their divine calling. Similarly, extend your prayers to encompass your family's overall well-being, including their peace, prosperity, and spiritual health.

Daily prayer for yourself, your partner, and your family is not merely a suggestion but a vital responsibility. Embrace prayer as a steadfast companion that can move mountains and dispel challenges. Committing to earnest and frequent prayer will shield your family from spiritual adversaries and foster a nurturing and resilient environment for your marriage and loved ones.

For parents, prayer for their children is not optional but urgent. The enemy often targets children at a young age to influence their values and beliefs. Through prayer, we seek God's wisdom and protection over our children, asking Him to instill virtues such as character, love, joy, and self-confidence in them. Inviting God into their lives provides a strong spiritual foundation supporting their overall well-being (mental, emotional, physical, professional, matrimonial, and academic) and growth into healthy, successful adults.

Teaching children to pray is equally important. By instilling in them the habit of prayer, we help them understand its significance and power. If children are not taught to value and practice prayer, they may struggle with its importance in their daily lives or as they face life's challenges independently. It is crucial to model and impart this practice early on to ensure they grow up with a strong spiritual foundation from which they will not depart when they grow up.

Prayer is necessary in marriage and should be practiced daily. Our adversary, Satan, aims to undermine the blessed unions God has given us. The most powerful weapon against the spiritual forces threatening our marriages is prayer. Through prayer, God unveils the deceptions and tactics the enemy employs against our relationships. When you commit to earnest and regular prayer for your marriage, challenges will diminish, allowing harmony to flourish. It's crucial to teach your children the significance of prayer and its power to combat not just marital issues but all of life's adversities. Instilling this understanding at a young age enables them to embrace prayer as a way of life, guiding them toward stability, joy, and peace in their journeys.

In conclusion, when the principles of marriage, as ordained by God, are earnestly embraced, they enrich and satisfy your marital journey. Central to this transformation is prioritizing a connection with God, inviting His guidance into the path of your marriage. Virtues such as forgiveness, commitment, love, respect, empathy, fidelity, selflessness, and a mutual understanding of gender roles emerge as pivotal factors in fostering a profoundly fulfilling marriage. Melissa Ringstaff nicely summarizes this section: "Marriage is a beautiful and complex journey that requires dedication, hard work, and a deep commitment to love and respect."[55]

55. Melissa Ringstaff, "How to Show Your Husband Respect," *A Virtuous Woman*, Last modified February 23, 2023, Accessed January 14, 2023, https://avirtuouswoman.org/how-to-show-your-husband-respect/.

PART II

PRACTICAL ADVICE

CHAPTER IV

IMPLEMENTING FOUNDATIONAL PRINCIPLES

I n Western society individuals often rush into love but are equally quick to exit when faced with challenges and complexities. They may conveniently forget the solemn vows exchanged during their wedding ceremonies, when they pledged to stand by each other through thick and thin for a lifetime. Many fail to grasp marriage's foundational principles and duties and lack the perseverance to navigate its inevitable difficulties. Marriage necessitates a lifelong dedication to one another, yet in our contemporary culture, commitment is often undervalued, and people are reluctant to commit themselves to anything fully. As Clark Warren aptly puts it:

> Commitment asks a thousand more of you than just to stay in the marriage! It asks you to love, honor, and cherish the other person. It means avoiding a substitute spouse of any kind. It requires that you do everything in your

power to be all that your role requires of you. And it asks that you do all of this through every kind of circumstance for as long as you live. This kind of commitment has simply not been understood in our society.[56]

The essential marital principles can be learned and applied if you really want to build a fulfilling marriage. Here are a few we will develop.

COMMIT TO YOUR SPOUSE

Commitment stands as the cornerstone of any marriage, providing a profound source of joy and fulfillment. From a biblical perspective, this commitment is far more than just a matter of convenience or fleeting sentiment; it represents a sacred and binding covenant established before God. This covenant is intended to last a lifetime, mirroring the unending nature of God's promises to His people. When you enter marriage, you make a steadfast, lifelong commitment, not just a temporary arrangement. Commitment is indispensable to a thriving marriage. As John Maxwell says, "Just like anything else worth fighting for, marriage requires daily discipline and commitment."

Unfortunately, contemporary culture often undermines this concept, favoring selfishness over enduring commitment. In today's world, there's a tendency to approach marriage with a "let's give it a try" attitude, with the option to bail out when things get tough. This mindset significantly reduces your willingness to navigate the highs and lows of marriage. However, by honoring the divine covenant of marriage, which is meant to last "till death do us part," you lay a stronger foundation for a successful and enduring relationship.

---

56. Neil Clark Warren, *Finding the Love of Your Life: Ten Principles for Choosing the Right Marriage Partner* (Colorado Springs: Focus on the Family Publishing, 1992), 133.

Total faithfulness is another crucial element of marital commitment. It means dedicating yourself to honoring both the Lord and your spouse by remaining loyal throughout your life. Although temptation is a natural and inevitable part of being human, it's vital to remember your vows when faced with such challenges. Strengthen yourself by proactively avoiding situations and people that might tempt you. While everyone has personal strengths and weaknesses, recognizing and addressing potential sources of temptation is pivotal for maintaining faithfulness.

Commitment also entails avoiding the trap of divorce as a first response. While there are circumstances where divorce may be a last resort after all efforts have failed, it should never be the initial solution when facing difficulties. The true essence of marital commitment is to work through challenges and avoid divorce whenever possible. This perspective reflects the depth of your commitment to the marriage covenant and your determination to overcome obstacles. Remember, commitment is a choice, and choosing to work through challenges is also a deliberate choice you make for your marriage.

Moreover, genuine care for each other is a crucial aspect of commitment. This care should come naturally, driven by love and admiration, rather than merely fulfilling obligations or duties. It involves meeting each other's basic needs and addressing personal desires and wishes, ensuring both partners feel valued and appreciated. Love, at the core of this care, can overcome all obstacles, providing reassurance and confidence in the strength of your relationship.

Ultimately, marriage is about a deep commitment to love and care, staying faithful to your spouse until death, and honoring every aspect of the marriage covenant. Embracing this commitment brings your relationship true fulfillment, joy, stability, and satisfaction. This steadfast dedication allows a marriage to thrive and endure, reflecting the divine intention of a lifelong partnership. The joy and fulfillment that commitment brings to a marriage is truly inspiring and should motivate you to nurture your relationship.

PREPARE YOURSELF
BEFORE GETTING MARRIED

Preparing yourself before entering marriage is fundamental to ensuring a successful and fulfilling partnership. While being fully prepared for every aspect of marriage is impossible, taking proactive measures can significantly enhance your readiness for the journey ahead. Marriage is a dynamic and ongoing learning experience, requiring continuous effort and adaptation. To lay a strong foundation, it's intelligent to understand the implications of marriage and the commitment it entails. This understanding helps you engage with your spouse more effectively and build a solid relationship.

An integral part of preparation involves gaining a deep understanding of your partner. This means exploring what brings them happiness and fulfillment, as well as their concerns and fears. Discussing their life goals, relationship expectations, and sources of empowerment is crucial. You will be better equipped to support and serve your partner by grasping these variables. A thorough understanding of each other's values and vulnerabilities can help reduce potential conflicts and strengthen your connection as you navigate life together.

Equally important is assessing how you and your partner handle various aspects of life and marriage. Consider how you approach family responsibilities, economic activities, and personal development. Addressing potential issues, such as financial management or communication challenges, before they arise can prevent misunderstandings and create a more harmonious relationship. By discussing and preparing for these elements, you can build a resilient relationship capable of overcoming obstacles.

Furthermore, preparation should also encompass understanding the broader aspects of family life. This includes acknowledging the impact of societal and psychological factors on your relationship. Familiarize yourself with family dynamics, parenting challenges, in-laws, and the moral and psychological environments that influence your interactions. These elements can help you navigate complex situations more efficiently and contribute to a healthier family life.

Preparing for marriage also requires thoroughly examining other aspects of your life and relationship. This can be aligning your life goals, priorities, and objectives with your fiancé or fiancée. Differing goals can undermine unity and lead to disunion. It's crucial to ensure that you both have a *shared purpose*. Without a shared purpose, your marriage might lack meaning and a solid foundation, much like an aircraft without kerosene would fail to take flight despite its excellent design. Shared purpose acts as the vital fuel for a serious relationship. Just as you wouldn't consider a friendship genuine without common ground, a marriage without shared goals can deteriorate.

For believers in Christ, prayer is a fundamental part of preparation. Given the seriousness of this life project, it's wise to spend time in prayer, seeking God's guidance. Before making any significant decisions or taking steps forward, consult with your spiritual Father, the Lord Jesus. By putting Him first, you invite His guidance and strength into every step of your journey. He will support, protect, inspire, and help you navigate inevitable challenges. Praying together with your fiancé or fiancée before marriage will deepen your spiritual bond and align your relationship with divine purpose.

Another crucial area to discuss is lifestyle choices related to physical health and well-being. Talk about the habits you need to develop for maintaining a healthy lifestyle, such as proper nutrition and regular exercise. Address any existing health issues openly. If one of you is struggling with a health problem, this must be disclosed and discussed thoroughly. Understanding each other's health needs and preferences is vital to effectively supporting one another's wellness.

Adaptability is also vital. When single, you each lived unique lifestyles suited to your individual needs. Marriage will require expejustments, as you blend your separate experiences into a shared life. Be prepared to lower your expectations and adapt to new realities. Flexibility, resilience, and empathy will help you navigate these changes smoothly. A positive mindset and the ability to adjust to your new reality are fundamental for sustaining a harmonious marriage.

Educational and professional aspirations are another critical topic. Discuss how you both value work and how it will impact your marriage. Discuss the timing, funding, and support needed if you plan to pursue higher education. Balance work and life priorities to avoid conflicts that could strain your relationship. Ensuring you're both on the same page regarding career and education will help manage expectations and responsibilities.

Premarital counseling is highly recommended as it provides valuable guidance and prepares you for the realities of marriage. Although some may view it as unnecessary, having an experienced counselor to help navigate your transition into marriage can be highly beneficial. Counseling can address potential issues and equip you with tools to build a strong foundation.

Financial planning is another critical aspect of pre-marriage preparation. Discuss every detail related to finances, including money management styles, spending habits, saving practices, investments, and credit card usage. As a financial advisor, I've seen firsthand how financial disagreements strain relationships. Thorough financial planning will help prevent conflicts and ensure you understand your financial goals and practices clearly.

Finally, consider your family and friendship dynamics. Share details about how your family functions and what they mean to you. Address how you want your family and friends to be involved in your life moving forward. Clear communication about family and social expectations will help prevent surprises and disappointments, ensuring a smoother integration of your social networks into your married life.

Putting in the time and effort into preparing for marriage is a bright and practical approach to building a successful relationship. By focusing on individual and shared goals, understanding each other's needs, and proactively addressing potential challenges, you can lay a solid foundation for a lasting and fulfilling marriage. This preparation enhances your readiness for marriage and equips you with the tools needed to foster a supportive and loving partnership.

NURTURE EMOTIONAL WELL-BEING

Emotions have no intellect. Nurturing emotional well-being is crucial in maintaining a healthy marriage. It's natural for everyone to experience negative emotions occasionally, but it's important not to let these feelings dictate your actions. Instead, take proactive steps to manage your negative emotions. Acknowledging and addressing them constructively prevents these feelings from escalating and undermining your relationship. This approach ensures that your relationship remains strong and resilient, even when faced with emotional challenges.

Negative emotions accumulate and, if unchecked, can erode your commitment to your marital promises. It is important to constantly assess and address any discontent or frustration before they grow into deeper issues. Unmet needs and unfulfilled expectations can lead to resentment and negatively affect your relationship. By staying attentive to these emotional factors and addressing them quickly, you can prevent them from damaging your bond with your partner.

Maintaining control over your emotions is vital to preserving your sense of joy, peace, and tranquility in the relationship. Avoid allowing feelings of contempt, anger, or disdain to take root and disrupt your marital harmony. Instead, focus on fostering positive interactions and mutual understanding. Regularly engaging in open communication and addressing concerns can help keep your emotional well-being in check, ensuring your relationship remains fulfilling and supportive.

KEEPING THE SPARK ALIVE AND JOYFUL

Maintaining a vibrant and joyful marriage demands ongoing, intentional effort. Over time, the initial excitement that characterized the early stages of marriage naturally evolves into routine and familiarity. This shift isn't a sign of failure but an opportunity to renew your connection and deepen your bond. Investing in your relationship by consciously engaging in activities that strengthen your commitment can keep your marriage dynamic and fulfilling.

Maintaining a solid commitment to each other is one of the most critical aspects of sustaining a thriving relationship. As the novelty of early romance fades, it's recommended to prioritize your marriage amidst life's demands. Setting aside quality time for each other, being appreciative, and nurturing affection are vital practices. These efforts help prevent the relationship from becoming stagnant and ensuring your connection remains robust and lively.

In addition to revitalizing commitment, exploring new ways to connect with each other can infuse excitement into your marriage. Engaging in new hobbies, planning date nights, or embarking on novel experiences together can reignite your enthusiasm. These shared activities allow you to rediscover each other's passions and create lasting memories, fostering a sense of adventure and intimacy.

Equally important is maintaining focus and determination when addressing conflicts. Resolving issues with empathy and open communication is crucial for keeping the relationship healthy. By proactively tackling challenges and working through problems together, you reinforce your dedication to one another and strengthen your marital bond.

Deepening your emotional and spiritual connection further enriches your marriage. Beyond physical affection, understanding and supporting each other's needs and aspirations is vital. Engaging in meaningful conversations, active listening, and shared spiritual practices, such as prayer or studying the Word of God, can enhance intimacy and provide a strong foundation for your relationship.

Creativity also plays a significant role in keeping the marriage lively. Experimenting with innovative ways to express love, such as thoughtful gestures, personalized rituals, or setting mutual goals, can refresh your relationship. Seeking external support, like marriage enrichment programs or counseling, may offer new perspectives and tools to maintain a joyful and resilient marriage.

Daniel Richard highlights that the initial attraction that draws people together often diminishes over time. To sustain a deep level of love and commitment, couples must develop basic skills like trust, discipline, and goodwill. These qualities are cultivated through persistent effort and dedication, and they form the cornerstone of a lasting, passionate relationship.[57]

Staying connected to your partner's evolving interests and needs is not just important, it's crucial. You can maintain a strong and responsive relationship by regularly updating your understanding of their goals, desires, and daily experiences. This ongoing engagement is critical in ensuring that your connection remains meaningful and supportive as you grow and change.

Keeping your relationship alive and enjoyable is not a one-dimensional task. It involves a multifaceted approach. By focusing on commitment, exploring new connections, addressing conflicts with determination, deepening emotional intimacy, and embracing creativity, couples can foster a marriage that continues to bring joy and fulfillment. Continuous attention to each other's evolving needs and interests will ensure your relationship remains vibrant and resilient.

CULTIVATING A GROWTH MINDSET IN MARRIAGE

A marriage can't thrive if neither partner is willing to have a growth-oriented mindset. A fixed mindset leads to stagnation. Stagnation leads to feelings of depression, frustration, and resentment. If you're not ready to put in the work to grow together, you might be better off not engaging in the marriage adventure. Both partners must be committed to achieving the transformative growth necessary for a healthy marriage. You're meant to make each other stronger and better versions of yourselves through genuine effort to grow daily.

---

57. Daniel Richard, "Starving Marriage: Seven Recipes for Nourishing Intimacy" (PhD diss., Liberty University, April 2017), 10, https://digitalcommons.liberty.edu/doctoral/1385.

Remember that you're both imperfect individuals and that conflict is normal in marriage. In fact, conflict is a growth catalyst if you embrace it constructively. Things won't stay the same as when you first met even when you're both willing to work hard. Life goes through different seasons, each requiring daily effort to make your relationship work. Remember, fairy tales (movies) are just stories meant to entertain, not reflect reality. Love alone isn't enough; you have to give, not just receive.

Building a stable, healthy relationship takes skill—like communicating your needs clearly, navigating tough conversations, and knowing how to handle disagreements respectfully. These skills aren't just handed to you; they're developed over time through experience. So, when you marry, do so with the intention to grow rather than wanting to stay the same forever.

BUILD YOUR MARRIAGE ON UNCONDITIONAL LOVE, NOT CONDITIONAL EXPECTATIONS

In today's world, many couples fall into the trap of conditional love, driven by self-interest rather than genuine commitment. Too often, relationships are centered around personal gain rather than mutual support. Conditional love thrives on self-serving motives; it's the expectation that your partner will meet your needs and desires rather than entering the relationship with a readiness to serve and support each other.

When expectations are unmet, such a mindset makes it easy to consider ending the relationship at the first sign of difficulty. This approach reveals a fundamental lack of commitment and a willingness to abandon the marriage when challenges arise rather than working through them.

The driving force behind a strong and lasting relationship should be a deep commitment to loving and caring for your spouse unconditionally. This is the foundation of a strong and lasting relationship. Life is replete with challenges and obstacles, and marriage is no exception. If you're prepared to tolerate difficulties in other areas of life—such as dealing with an unpleasant neighbor, boss, friend, challenging colleagues, or tough situations in your environment (be it political, social, or cultural)—but unwilling to extend the same tolerance and commitment to your spouse, it indicates a significant issue. A genuine commitment to marriage involves embracing both the highs and lows with equal dedication and compassion.

Cultivating unconditional love should be seen as a life goal, and serving someone you love brings a profound sense of fulfillment. Love leads to a transformative and enriching experience when practiced intentionally and freely. Unconditional love is characterized by its willingness and positive intent, meaningfully transforming both the giver and the receiver. By pursuing this form of love daily, you can experience genuine joy and contentment from nurturing a relationship grounded in mutual respect and commitment.

Mipo asserts that marriage relationships are not thriving in today's society. The once most valued and cherished human-to-human relationship has lost its hunger and has been cheapened to an association with conditions. The world that is focused on self has brought destructive ideas to a sacred relationship based on God's gift to mankind. When a couple is only concerned with meeting their own individual needs and not motivated to help each other, anger and selfishness begin to creep into the marriage bond.[58]

Focusing on unconditional love rather than conditional expectations is crucial to building a strong marriage. Entering the relationship

---

58. Mipo, "Social Relations and Implications on Families in Africa."

with a readiness to support and care for your spouse, regardless of challenges, is important. This mindset ensures that both partners are committed to working through difficulties together, leading to a more fulfilling and resilient union. Embracing unconditional love as a daily practice enriches the relationship and transforms both partners, creating a lasting and profoundly satisfying bond.

RESPECTING EACH OTHER MUTUALLY

Mutual respect is not just a nice-to-have in a successful relationship; it's a must-have, especially in marriage. It's the bedrock of a strong partnership, helping couples weather storms and keep their bond intact. When respect is present, it's a sturdy platform that aids partners in tackling challenges together. But when respect fades, the relationship suffers, often beyond repair. That's why I've repeatedly stressed the importance of respect in this book. The truth is that very few marriages can survive without mutual respect.

Respect is not just a fleeting sentiment; it is a fundamental aspect of one's character. It shapes how we view and interact with others. When respect diminishes, we start to see the other person with disdain, undervaluing their worth and importance. This shift in perspective can lead to feelings of disregard and even contempt, turning the relationship sour. In romantic relationships, losing respect means that any positive qualities previously admired become overshadowed by negativity, making the relationship feel hollow and unfulfilling.

It is crucial to be vigilant about signs of declining respect in your relationship. If you start to notice feelings of disregard or contempt creeping in, it is clever to address these issues promptly. Even if you struggle to find something admirable about your partner in challenging times, there is always some aspect worth respecting.

For instance, you can appreciate their dedication to their work or their kindness towards others. Focus on that positive element and let it guide your interactions. Often, respect wanes because we fail to recognize and appreciate the positives, allowing the negative aspects to overshadow the relationship. You can prevent it from fading by paying attention and consciously maintaining respect.

Life's circumstances will shape who you meet, and your heart will decide who stays in your life. However, character—embodied by respect—determines the quality of your relationships. Unlike knowledge, which can be fleeting and fallible, character remains steadfast. Respect is a crucial element of character, and it is wise to cultivate and preserve it in your marriage. By prioritizing respect, you ensure your marriage remains strong and capable of enduring life's trials.

Respect is often said to be *earned*; but in a marriage, waiting for your spouse to earn your respect can prevent you from fully engaging in the relationship. If you hold back respect until your spouse meets your expectations, you miss the opportunity to act selflessly and nurture your marriage. Genuine respect should be given freely and consistently, not withheld until it is "earned."

In a healthy marriage, respect must be a mutual and daily practice, regardless of the circumstances. Even when faced with difficulties, maintaining respect is crucial. What may seem like a significant problem in your marriage could be a challenge others wish they had. The notion that "the grass is greener on the other side" reflects a common temptation to compare our relationships to others. Every marriage faces challenges; the outcome depends on how you manage them. Always respecting your spouse builds a foundation that supports and strengthens your marriage.

During a conversation with a couple celebrating their 50th

wedding anniversary, I was struck by their enduring and joyful marriage. When I asked about the key to their success, their answer was simple yet profound: "Respect." They elaborated, emphasizing that they had never ceased to show respect to each other, regardless of the circumstances. "Whether facing arguments, challenges, moments of joy or sadness, mutual respect remained a constant reality of our behavior towards one another." Their milestone anniversary is a testament to the power of respect in a marriage.

This insight was enlightening for me, showing the significance of respect in sustaining a marriage. Respect often dissipates during conflict, ironically when it is most needed. Sadly, many couples quickly resort to disrespectful behavior during disagreements. However, it is crucial to remember the importance of maintaining respect, especially during conflict and misunderstanding. Cultivating mutual respect strengthens a marriage's stability, health, and fulfillment.

Mutual respect is indispensable for a thriving marriage. It provides a solid foundation that helps partners face challenges together and maintain a healthy relationship. Respect is a core aspect of character, so it must be actively nurtured and preserved. By focusing on respect, you reinforce the strength and endurance of your marriage, ensuring that it remains resilient and fulfilling through all of life's ups and downs.

EMBRACE HONESTY AND OPENNESS IN YOUR MARRIAGE

Embracing honesty and openness in marriage is not just important; it's necessary for building a solid and enduring relationship. Lies can deeply wound a loving and committed spouse; and not every healthy relationship can withstand deception. If you find yourself lying or hiding the truth from your partner, you must stop this behavior immediately.

Lies undermine trust, and once trust is compromised, respect inevitably follows. Without respect, the foundation of your relationship becomes unstable, making it extremely difficult to rebuild. Therefore, it is smart to prioritize honesty and transparency in your marriage. Remember, lies cannot be hidden forever; eventually, they will come to light, often causing greater damage than if the truth had been revealed from the start.

Truthfulness might seem like a fundamental aspect of a relationship, yet many individuals struggle to maintain it consistently. When lies are uncovered, the impact can be profoundly hurtful and may threaten the very fabric of the relationship. Trust, once broken, is challenging to restore, and the emotional scars left by deception can linger long after the truth is revealed. Therefore, maintaining a commitment to honesty is not just a matter of principle but a necessity for the health of the marriage.

If you have concerns about how your spouse might react to certain truths, it's better to address these issues openly rather than resorting to dishonesty. Finding constructive ways to express your concerns allows for mutual understanding and adjustments that can enhance the relationship. One practical way to foster honesty and transparency is through regular communication. Your feelings and concerns with your partner create an open and honest environment crucial for a fulfilling and lasting marriage.

As relationship expert Gary Chapman wisely noted, "Becoming an authentically loving person calls for putting off the practice of lying and putting on the practice of truth-telling." [59] This approach is

---

59. Chapman, *Love as a Way of Life*, 168.

key for nurturing a genuine and supportive relationship. By embracing truthfulness, you align your actions with the values of trust and respect, which are vital for a strong marriage.

Honesty and transparency are cornerstones of a successful marriage. Lies may offer temporary relief, but they ultimately erode the trust and respect necessary for a healthy relationship. Committing to truth-telling strengthens the bond between partners and fosters a deeper, more fulfilling connection. By prioritizing honesty, you build a resilient foundation for your marriage, ensuring it remains strong and enduring all life's challenges.

TRANSPARENT COMMUNICATION AND MUTUAL UNDERSTANDING

Addressing sensitive topics within a marriage can be daunting, especially when it involves pointing out perceived weaknesses or discussing challenging issues. Conversations about personal addictions and struggles, body weight, financial management, or unhealthy personal attitudes often provoke discomfort and fear. Many couples avoid these difficult discussions to maintain a semblance of peace and tranquility. However, avoiding these crucial conversations can lead to unresolved issues that undermine the relationship over time. Wisdom lies in confronting these realities with honesty and understanding that open communication is vital for the health of the marriage.

Establishing mutual understanding and fostering effective communication are foundational elements of what I refer to as "Healthy Marital Accountability." This approach involves discussing uncomfortable truths with compassion and respect. It's humble to address issues while acknowledging one's own mistakes and being open to personal growth. By embracing this level of transparency and commitment to improvement, couples can strengthen their bond and create a more supportive and resilient relationship.

The challenge often arises from the fear of causing hurt or conflict by sharing uncomfortable truths. Many people avoid expressing their true feelings, especially on sensitive topics, to prevent emotional pain. Unfortunately, this avoidance can lead to a buildup of unresolved issues, which may later surface during heated arguments, causing further damage. Addressing issues in a non-confrontational manner and a calm setting helps prevent feelings of betrayal or attack and fosters a healthier dialogue. As Leigh and Clark contend, "Good communication can be difficult at times."[60]

Ultimately, being honest with your spouse about complex subjects while maintaining a respectful and empathetic approach is crucial for a solid and enduring relationship. This practice helps prevent the accumulation of unspoken grievances and promotes a deeper connection. By prioritizing transparent communication and mutual understanding, married couples can navigate challenges more effectively and build a relationship grounded in trust and respect.

FINANCIAL PLANNING

Conflicts in marriages often stem from various sources, but financial issues are frequently at the forefront. Establishing a strong financial plan is vital to mitigating these disputes. By creating a budget and making joint decisions on spending and investments, couples can significantly reduce financial tension. This proactive strategy fosters a sense of stability and relief and lays the groundwork for a more

---

60. Sharon J. Leigh and Janet A. Clark, "Human Relations: Creating a Strong and Satisfying Marriage," *MU Extension*, 2000, https://extension.missouri.edu/media/wysiwyg/Extensiondata/Pub/pdf/hesguide/humanrel/gh6610.pdf.

harmonious future. Financial disagreements can become a persistent problem if one partner feels the other is mismanaging or overspending. Such conflicts will persist until they are addressed together with a clear plan.

If couples neglect to plan their finances, they risk jeopardizing their future. Every expense and financial decision is interconnected, and without a structured plan, there's no clear path or direction for managing money effectively. This emphasizes the benefit of open and honest communication about financial habits and expectations. By engaging in transparent discussions and making collective financial decisions, couples can prevent or resolve conflicts and ensure a more secure and balanced future together.

As a financial planner, I've witnessed the challenges that arise when couples fail to manage their finances effectively. Many struggle to achieve their financial goals or prepare for retirement due to a lack of disciplined planning. However, couples can secure their financial future by adopting wise financial habits, such as controlled spending, prudent debt management, and collaborative investment decisions. This should instill a sense of motivation and determination in your marriage.

This emphasizes the significant benefits of financial planning for upholding the family's financial security, fostering psychological tranquility, and ensuring marital harmony. Establishing clear roles and maintaining accountability are crucial to achieving successful financial stability. As Leigh and Clark contribute:

> Regardless of the amount of money a couple has, it is often
> the biggest source of marital conflict. Husbands and wives
> often have very diverse ideas about how money should be

handled because they have experienced different family values and goals regarding money... Constructing a budget and financial planning often require negotiation and compromise, but they are important tasks and aid spouses in identifying their priorities and goals for the future.[61]

Let's dive deeper. In my work as a financial planner, I encourage couples to take charge of their finances, educate themselves, and learn how to manage their finances responsibly. Here are some strategies that can empower couples.

Establish Goals

Setting goals together fosters a sense of shared responsibility and helps couples hold each other accountable for their decisions. Goals can take the shape of short-term to long-term and may be ongoing, one-time, or seasonal. These may include accumulating funds for a vehicle, charitable gifting, or enduring financial endeavors such as funding day-to-day expenses, retirement, or savings for children's education. For example, planning for the down payment or monthly mortgage payments is prudent if you're aiming to buy a house. Ensure your salaries align with the type of house you intend to purchase to avoid financial strain.

Budget and Plan Expenses Together

Active participation from both partners in the budgeting process is crucial. Many couples who neglect financial planning find themselves unprepared when faced with unexpected expenses or changes in circumstances. Budgeting should align with realistic, achievable

---

61. Leigh, and Clark, "Human Relations,."

goals, and both partners should agree on the budget to avoid over-spending. Without budgeting, it's easy to fall into debt and hinder progress toward future financial goals, such as helping the children with unexpected financial challenges, purchasing a desired item, retirement, or vacations.

Build Emergency Funds

Emergency funds are essential for meeting financial obligations during hardships such as job loss. It's recommended to save around six months' monthly expenses if one partner works and three months' worth if both partners make substantial income. Neglecting this precautionary measure can leave you vulnerable when unexpected crises occur and lead to dire and stressful situations that are difficult to navigate. Prioritize building your emergency fund before planning to save for other ventures or projects.

Manage Debt Wisely

Avoid accumulating unnecessary debt. Prioritize paying off high-interest loans first until all high-interest loans are paid off. Once debts are paid off, refrain from renewing the cycle and focus on saving instead. Debt should serve as a tool, not a destination. It's crucial to align your expenses with your income and live within your means. Strive to refrain from exceeding your earnings through prudent spending habits.

For some couples, relying on credit cards becomes a recurring pattern, evolving into a lifestyle that requires diligent efforts to reverse. Avoid finding yourself in this predicament, and if you're already trapped, take immediate steps to extricate yourself. Adopting debt as a lifestyle is not a matter of pride. Debt traps you in servitude to the lender, relinquishing your autonomy. Seize control of your financial affairs and reclaim your independence. By doing so, you're not just taking charge of your money but also securing your future and that of your loved ones.

Save

Successful couples prioritize saving and adhere to strategies such as the 50/30/20 formula (50% needs, 30% wants, 20% savings). Saving 10-20% of your salary for future expenses, including retirement and children's future, is crucial for financial stability. For instance, failure to save could result in an indefinite work period without the prospect of retirement. Cultivating a habit of saving is imperative for all couples, necessitating steadfast commitment and adherence. The sense of accomplishment and progress that come with saving and investing can be a powerful motivator for couples, inspiring them to stay on track with their financial goals.

For many individuals, saving proves challenging, as the array of needs often appears insurmountable, surpassing the capacity to set aside funds. If you find yourself in this situation, understand that there will always be temptations to spend. Consider establishing automatic withdrawals, a process where a fixed amount is deducted from your salary and channeled into your retirement, savings, or retail accounts. By automating this process, you can effectively boost your savings rate. Moreover, when you experience a salary increase, prioritize enhancing your automatic saving mechanism to pay yourself first.

Some may argue against saving, especially if they don't have specific future goals and objectives. Why sacrifice present enjoyment for an uncertain future? However, it's crucial to recognize that saving isn't solely about achieving particular goals but building a financial safety net. Failing to save leaves one vulnerable to unforeseen financial emergencies, perpetuating dependency on debt. Therefore, planning, saving diligently, and seizing opportunities to increase wealth is wise. Remember, tomorrow is uncertain, but you have control over today.

Invest

Investment proves important in people's lives. No matter your experience in investing, beginning with modest investments and utilizing tax-advantaged vehicles such as Roth IRAs can be a game-changer. This approach empowers you to take control of your financial future, ensuring you optimize tax-free withdrawals upon retirement, and even allows you to pass on tax-free funds to your children with no requirements to take the "Required Minimum Distributions" when you turn a certain age.

Moreover, fully utilizing employer-sponsored plans such as 401(k), 457, 403(b), SEP IRA and Simple IRA are essential to harness tax-deferred growth potential. By minimizing taxable income and maximizing growth through these plans, you're essentially capitalizing on free money from your employer. Ignoring such an opportunity is imprudent, especially considering the importance of retirement savings. You can amass significant wealth using these methods, as the compounding effect demonstrates its potency in savings.

Let me illustrate with a practical scenario. Imagine you're 25 years old, regularly saving and investing $200 monthly, with an anticipated annual return of 7%. If you maintain this approach by reaching 65, the initial $96,000 in your portfolio could potentially grow to $512,700. This example vividly demonstrates the efficacy of investing and the enduring impact of long-term compounding.

Many young married couples overlook the significance of early retirement savings, mistakenly assuming they have ample time before retirement. However, commencing savings early in life provides the assurance of a secure and fulfilling retirement. As Harry Emerson once said, "Don't retire from something; retire to something." Insufficient retirement funds often lead to tension among couples during retirement, as they struggle to maintain their previous lifestyle or afford desired luxuries. Thinking ahead and initiating savings early on is crucial, as even small contributions can yield significant returns when invested wisely. It may be advantageous to consider evaluating your insurance coverage.

Evaluate Insurance Coverage

Make certain your insurance coverage is neither excessive nor insufficient. If you're raising young children, consider securing Term Life insurance to provide for them in the event of an unexpected loss. Assess the adequacy of your disability coverage and review your homeowner's, umbrella, and personal auto policies for sufficient protection.

Ensure Equal Contribution to Financial Obligations Deepens Intimacy and Provides a Fair Distribution of Responsibilities.

Equitable accountability can always be maintained regardless of income discrepancies or employment status. Each partner should bear the same level of responsibility for managing the household finances. For instance, commitment and dedication from both sides are required when prioritizing retirement savings.

Communicate Openly

In discussions or planning concerning finances, avoiding developing any taboos between spouses is crucial. Each partner should feel comfortable and valued for openly expressing their expectations, aspirations, and financial goals. This level of transparency fosters shared responsibility, strengthens the connection between partners, and cultivates collaboration and optimism for the future. Open communication in financial matters is key to feeling understood and connected in your relationship.

If challenges arise in managing finances, it's important not to suppress communication or hinder the expression of expectations and concerns. Instead, work together to establish a disciplined approach that adheres to mutually agreed-upon plans. Financial issues often pose significant challenges in marriages, regardless of wealth status. Therefore, sincere and caring communication about all financial matters is clever. It can also be beneficial to consider home ownership.

Homeownership as a Couple Can Be a Wise Financial Decision

Various factors like your financial situation (income and assets), lifestyle preferences, and long-term goals can influence your decision. Regardless of your goals, if you plan adequately, consider owning a home. The benefits of homeownership, such as building equity and providing stability, a way to avoid heavy concentration of investment in one pile (called diversification) can be motivating factors in this decision.

When you own a home and make mortgage payments, you're not just paying off a loan. You're building equity, which can accumulate substantial wealth over time, making homeownership a smart financial move. Real estate has traditionally been a solid long-term investment, with property values generally appreciating over time, potentially increasing the value of your home. Homeownership allows for personal customization of your living space, from renovations to decorations, without landlord restrictions. It also offers various tax benefits, such as deductions on mortgage interest and property taxes, leading to significant savings.

Additionally, owning a home can enhance your sense of community and belonging, as you're more likely to form lasting connections with neighbors. Despite the initial costs, homeownership often proves more cost-effective than renting over time, serving as a valuable asset that diversifies your financial portfolio. It complements other investments like stocks, bonds, and business holdings by providing stability and potential long-term growth. Furthermore, owning a home can enrich your estate, a tax-efficient way to transfer assets to your heirs, particularly in community property states where they benefit from a full step-up in basis.

Homeownership is a financial investment that can provide stability, security, and peace. It's knowing that you have a place to call your own, free from the uncertainties of sudden rent increases or the whims of a landlord. It's a sanctuary that provides a sense of calm and reassurance, a place where you can truly relax and be yourself.

Keep Separate Accounts When Necessary

When necessary, it's advisable to maintain individual accounts. This suggestion might seem unconventional or peculiar, but in cases where attempts to align spending habits with an agreed-upon budget fail, separating bank accounts could salvage the situation. Keeping finances separate while collectively managing household expenses and responsibilities could eliminate conflicts altogether.

As a financial advisor, I've queried numerous couples on navigating financial disagreements, tensions, and mismanagement. The recurring and most impactful solution has been maintaining separate finances.

One couple shared a poignant testimony: "We've been married for forty-four years now." In the initial three years, financial disputes were incessant and heated. The wife admitted, "I was spending on clothes and anything I desired to purchase without a second thought. However, since segregating our bank accounts, not only has this issue ceased, but our conflicts overall have diminished. All our disagreements stemmed from spending habits. Over the past forty-one years, we've enjoyed a content and harmonious marriage."

While separating accounts can be a viable solution, it's crucial to understand the potential challenges. The risk of a dishonest partner misusing funds for their own benefit is a valid concern. However, these risks can be effectively managed with open communication and mutual accountability, providing a sense of security and making separate accounts a feasible option for some couples.

Keep Joint Accounts When Both Partners Are Responsible

When both partners are responsible, accountable, and disciplined about sticking to agreed-upon budgets and plans, keeping joint accounts can be beneficial. This approach streamlines transactions and simplifies household financial management. At the same time, maintaining individual accounts for personal spending is a good idea. This allows each person to make discretionary purchases—such as birthday gifts or small treats—without asking for permission, which can sometimes be uncomfortable.

The key is to choose a strategy that balances personal freedom with the collective financial security of the household, ensuring that both partners can manage their finances effectively without negative consequences. Ultimately, the key is to adopt strategies that best suit the dynamics of your marriage. What works for one couple may not be suitable for another; therefore, choosing approaches that resonate with both partners is intelligent, ensuring a harmonious and fulfilling relationship.

Celebrate Progress and Successes

Acknowledging and celebrating your small victories and progress towards achieving your goals and objectives is vital. It's rational not to focus solely on reaching your goals without taking the time to celebrate your successes along the way. For instance, if one partner has overcome a spending issue by becoming more mindful of their expenses, praising their efforts and recognizing their dedication to making positive changes is important. When working towards a savings goal, it's beneficial to celebrate milestones reached along the journey. Life should be embraced and celebrated as it unfolds while also maintaining gratitude for what you have and striving to make continual improvements each day.

SPENDING QUALITY TIME TOGETHER

Investing significant time in each other's company is a luxury necessary for healthy and thriving relationships. Far from being a mere luxury, spending quality time together is a fundamental practice that deepens emotional connections and enhances intimacy. This practice extends beyond physical presence for Christian couples, fostering spiritual intimacy, mutual support, and emotional depth. Engaging in shared activities and experiences strengthens the marital bond and reinforces the relationship's spiritual and emotional aspects.

Quality time in a Christian marriage can take various forms, such as praying together, studying the Bible, attending church services, and engaging in meaningful conversations about faith and life. These activities promote spiritual growth and create opportunities for couples to connect more deeply. For instance, praying together before bed or discussing a Bible verse over breakfast can be simple yet powerful ways to foster spiritual intimacy.

Additionally, participating in acts of service or ministry together, such as volunteering at a local shelter or leading a church group, can further strengthen the marital bond, as working together towards a common goal fosters mutual support and understanding.

Beyond spiritual practices, quality time includes dedicating full attention to each other through activities that both partners enjoy. This might involve dining out and savoring each other's company without the distractions of everyday life or participating in recreational activities that create lasting memories. Whether enjoying a quiet meal together or embarking on a fun adventure, these moments of undivided attention help reinforce the connection between spouses and contribute to a more fulfilling relationship.

Quality time, is a delightful source of joy and fulfillment that fortifies the marital bond. Whether it's a fun walk in the park, cooking a special meal together, or sharing a common hobby, these everyday activities are more than just ways to spend time. They are opportunities to connect, to share experiences, and to create lasting memories. Active pursuits like hiking, physical exercise, or exploring nature can bring a sense of adventure and shared accomplishment. Engaging in structured activities like attending marriage enrichment workshops, participating in community service, or planning a romantic getaway can enhance the relationship by offering new perspectives and experiences.

The benefits of quality time in a marriage extend beyond just spending time together. It has a profound impact on both the emotional and spiritual dimensions of the relationship. Couples who consistently invest time in each other will likely experience heightened intimacy and emotional stability. By setting aside distractions and focusing entirely on each other during these moments, couples can foster deeper emotional connections and strengthen relational intimacy, which, in turn, helps them navigate challenges more effectively.

Moreover, staying close physically, emotionally, and mentally contributes to a solid and enduring marital bond. Energetic intimacy, which refers to the shared energy and passion between partners, is supported by certain disciplines and characteristics, such as understanding the original purpose of marriage, maintaining open communication, and resolving conflicts positively. These traits, combined with spending quality time together and enjoying sexual intimacy, help build a resilient and committed relationship.

As Daniel affirms, "Quality time not only increases the spiritual bond but also has a huge impact on the emotional stability of a marriage relationship. Again, couples that spend thirty minutes or more of valuable time together are more likely to have heightened intimacy in all areas of their relationship."[62]

Investing quality time together is a vital practice for maintaining a thriving marriage. By engaging in shared activities, fostering spiritual and emotional intimacy, and setting aside distractions, couples can strengthen their bond and create lasting memories. This commitment to spending meaningful time together enhances the relationship and supports emotional stability and spiritual growth, reinforcing the foundation of a healthy and fulfilling marriage.

---

62. Richard, "Starving Marriage."

CULTIVATING FORGIVENESS

Forgiveness, while not always easy, has the power to transform a relationship. It's not about excusing or forgetting a transgression but healing and understanding. It's a process that requires both the person who has been hurt and the one who has caused the harm to engage in a compassionate and honest dialogue. When both parties are willing to release their grievances and offer compassion—and when wrongdoers acknowledge their mistakes and demonstrate a commitment to change—genuine reconciliation can occur. This transformative power of forgiveness gives hope for a brighter future in any relationship.

Understanding that everyone is fallible is vital to cultivating forgiveness. Even with the best intentions, people can unintentionally or inadvertently hurt their partners. Recognizing this inherent imperfection in human nature allows individuals to approach forgiveness with greater empathy and patience. By accepting that mistakes are part of being human, both partners can move towards forgiveness with a more realistic and compassionate perspective.

Forgiveness means releasing the urge for revenge and the negative emotions associated with the hurt. It requires the wronged individual to work through feelings and relinquish the need to hold onto resentment. This process of letting go is crucial for emotional healing and restoring trust. Additionally, forgiveness can lead to relational repair if the injured party chooses to reengage with the offender, aiming to rebuild a loving and trustworthy relationship. This effort involves both partners working together to overcome the transgression.

The process of forgiveness is not just about letting go of past grievances. We must dig to understand and address the underlying issues contributing to the wrongdoing. The person seeking forgiveness should try to understand the wrongdoer's background, life challenges, and limitations. This involves acknowledging their own relational faults and being open to dialogue about how both parties can improve. By fostering this mutual understanding and communication, couples can rebuild love and trust in their relationship.

Cultivating forgiveness is not a one-time event but a dynamic and ongoing process. It's a commitment to understanding, addressing, and overcoming the challenges that come with any relationship. By embracing forgiveness, individuals can heal emotional wounds, restore trust, and strengthen relationships. This commitment to forgiveness resolves past grievances and builds a more resilient and loving partnership for the future.

EXPEJUSTMENT: ADJUSTING EXPECTATIONS REALISTICALLY AND REASONABLY

One aspect of a healthy relationship is understanding and managing expectations. This is where the concept of "expejustment" comes in. It's about setting realistic, attainable, and reasonable expectations. By embracing expejustment, couples can navigate the complexities of marriage with greater understanding and love. It's a powerful tool that empowers both partners to manage disappointments and conflicts effectively, ensuring they feel valued and understood. Expectations naturally drive our desires and anticipations within a relationship.

However, when these expectations are unrealistic or not communicated effectively, they can become sources of significant frustration and disappointment. For example, if one partner anticipates constant romantic gestures while the other expresses love through everyday acts of service, unmet expectations can lead to emotional strain. Recognizing and addressing these mismatched expectations can prevent prolonged disappointment and contribute to a more satisfying relationship.

The role of expejustment (realistic expectations) cannot be overstated. Unrealistic demands, like expecting a spouse to fulfill all emotional needs or always exhibiting ideal behavior, can put undue pressure on the relationship. Consider a scenario where one partner expects the other to always prioritize family time over personal interests. When these expectations are unmet, the result can be a profound sense of neglect or undervaluation. By adjusting these expectations to align with practical realities, couples can better appreciate each other's contributions and reduce misunderstandings.

Approaching your spouse gracefully and kindly is prudent when expectations are unmet. Grace involves understanding and accepting your partner's limitations and imperfections, while kindness means communicating needs and feelings in a way that acknowledges their efforts and expresses appreciation. For instance, if your spouse forgets an important date, responding calmly and working together to find a solution maintains harmony.

Practical examples of expejustment include realistic communication and conflict resolution. No one can read minds, so expecting your spouse to know what you need without clear communication is unrealistic. Learn to have honest conversations about your needs and expectations. Similarly, conflicts are an inevitable part of any relationship. Rather than expecting a conflict-free marriage, focus on developing healthy strategies for resolving disagreements respectfully and constructively.

Personal growth is another aspect in which expejustment plays a crucial role. Both partners will evolve over time, so expecting immediate or drastic changes is unrealistic. Significant changes occur gradually, and accepting that your spouse's core characteristics will remain relatively unchanged is important. For example, expecting an extroverted spouse to become introverted is unreasonable and fails to appreciate their true nature. Accepting these inherent traits helps manage expectations and foster a more harmonious relationship. Miller and Tedder say, "As a general rule, accurate expectations will lead to smaller discrepancies between expectations and reality, while biased expectations will lead to larger discrepancies."[63]

To implement expejustment effectively, consider these strategies: (1) Engage in self-reflection to ensure your expectations are reasonable and not overly demanding. (2) Openly communicate your expectations with your spouse to ensure mutual understanding. (3) Be flexible, adapt your expectations as life circumstances change, and practice empathy by understanding your partner's perspective. Cultivating a positive attitude toward your spouse's efforts and focusing on strengths rather than shortcomings can also enhance relationship satisfaction.

Managing expectations through expejustment involves aligning anticipations with reality and approaching your partner with grace and understanding. By doing so, couples can build a stronger, more resilient relationship grounded in mutual respect, love, and empathy.

In essence, managing expectations through expejustment is about aligning your anticipations with reality and approaching your spouse with grace and understanding. Setting fair and reasonable expectations and communicating openly can prevent disappointment and build a stronger, more resilient marriage. This approach not only shields you from profound emotional wounds but also enhances the

---

63. Jessica Miller and Brandi Tedder, "The Discrepancy between Expectations and Reality: Satisfaction in Romantic Relationships" (class in PSY 401: Advanced Research at Hanover College, Hanover, IN, Fall 2011). https://psych.hanover.edu/research/Thesis12/papers/Millar%20Teddar%2Final%20Paper.pdf.

quality of your relationship, fostering a partnership that thrives on mutual respect, love, and empathy.

Expejustment is about setting expectations that are not only aspirational but also attainable and grounded in reality. By aligning expectations with biblical principles and practical realities, married couples can build a more fulfilling and harmonious relationship. This approach helps manage disappointment and strengthens the bond between spouses, allowing them to navigate the complexities of marriage with greater understanding and love.

MUTUAL UNDERSTANDING OF PERSPECTIVE

Understanding your partner's perspective is not just about acknowledging their point of view; it's about stepping into their shoes with empathy. Each individual brings unique experiences, cultural influences, and a personal background into the marriage. Disregarding these perspectives not only shows a lack of empathy but can also undermine the health of your relationship. To build a strong and supportive relationship, it's wise for couples to engage with and value the spouse's perspective actively. This empathetic understanding can lead to a more harmonious and fulfilling relationship filled with love and mutual respect.

Ignoring your partner's perspective can lead to significant issues within the marriage. Failing to empathize with your spouse's experiences and viewpoints can result in stubbornness and conflict. This absence of understanding can lead to feelings of isolation and frustration, potentially leading to more severe problems such as marital discord or infidelity. Consistently trying to understand and accept your partner's perspective is crucial for maintaining a harmonious relationship. For instance, not understanding your partner's perspective on a significant life decision could lead to resentment and a sense of being unheard, which can strain the relationship.

Constructive conflict resolution is not a mystery; it's a skill that can be honed through mutual understanding. Effective resolution of disagreements often hinges on both partners being willing to see the situation from each other's perspectives. When partners remain open to understanding differing viewpoints, they can address conflicts more productively and find solutions that respect both sides. This practice helps to prevent misunderstandings and recurring arguments, which can otherwise create a cycle of unresolved issues. By mastering this skill, you can take control of your relationship's dynamics and foster a more harmonious bond.

Research on perspective-taking in relationships has identified several key behaviors that contribute to positive interactions. Effective perspective-taking includes showing agreement, attentiveness, and making relevant contributions to conversations. It also involves maintaining a positive tone and allowing freedom in sharing personal experiences. Conversely, negative behaviors such as disagreement, inattentiveness, and constraining the partner's storytelling can indicate a lack of genuine perspective-taking. These findings emphasize the importance of engaging constructively with your partner's viewpoint.

In a recent survey I conducted, participants highlighted the significance of genuinely understanding their partner's perspective. Many noted that this insight was crucial for preventing conflicts and building stronger unity within the relationship. The survey revealed that making a sincere effort to comprehend each other's viewpoints helps reduce the frequency of disagreements and fosters a more cohesive and supportive partnership.

One couple shared a transformative experience that emphasized the value of perspective- taking. They recognized that understanding each other's viewpoints was pivotal for effective communication. This realization came as an "Aha!" moment, emphasizing the importance of empathy and the significant effort required to bridge gaps created by differing backgrounds and experiences. Focusing on perspective-taking enhanced their communication and strengthened their relationship, inspiring others to do the same.

Ultimately, conflicts will likely persist without a genuine understanding of your partner's perspective, and authentic connection may remain out of reach. However, by embracing and valuing each other's viewpoints, couples can build a more solid, resilient relationship grounded in mutual understanding and respect. This highlights the critical role of empathy and open communication in cultivating a lasting and harmonious marriage, offering hope and optimism to all couples.

THE ROLE OF SACRIFICE IN MARRIAGE

In all of this, one truth remains evident: life in general, and marriage specifically, is not and should not be motivated solely by pursuing self-fulfillment or expecting sacrifice-free relationships. The essence of a fulfilling marriage is not found in the quest for personal satisfaction alone but in the mutual commitment to giving and receiving through intentional sacrifice.

Sacrifice in marriage is often misunderstood. It is not about giving up everything you value or enduring undue hardship. Instead, it involves a conscious and willing decision to put your partner's needs and well-being alongside your own, creating a balance that fosters mutual benefit and deepens the connection between spouses. True sacrifice is about selflessly prioritizing your partner's happiness and the relationship's health, which ultimately nurtures your own sense of fulfillment and contentment.

By its very nature, marriage requires sacrifice. This doesn't mean that one partner should always give while the other only takes, but rather that both partners should be willing to expejust and compromise for the sake of the relationship. This mutual willingness to sacrifice is a cornerstone of a strong and lasting marriage, highlighting the commitment and dedication required from both partners.

An attitude focused solely on self-fulfillment or expecting relationships to be sacrifice- free can lead to dissatisfaction and disappointment. When each partner enters a marriage with the expectation of having their needs met without offering anything in return, the relationship becomes transactional rather than transformational. This approach often leads to a cycle of unmet expectations and unhappiness.

For example, if one partner expects the other to always cater to their needs without reciprocal support or understanding, it can create a lopsided dynamic. The partner who feels unappreciated may withdraw or become less engaged, leading to a breakdown in communication and intimacy. This cycle can erode trust and mutual respect, ultimately affecting the overall satisfaction within the marriage.

Intentional sacrifice is not just about making deliberate choices to benefit your partner and the relationship but also about reaping the rewards of a stronger, more fulfilling bond. Even when it involves personal inconvenience or compromise, this approach, based on the biblical principles of love and selflessness, can lead to a deeper connection. This sacrificial love is not about expecting something in return but about giving selflessly and unconditionally; the benefits are immeasurable.

A marriage that thrives on mutual fulfillment is rooted in the principle of intentional sacrifice. By embracing this mindset, couples can navigate the challenges of life and marriage with greater empathy and understanding. Sacrifice in marriage is not about erasing individual needs or desires but balancing them with a commitment to the relationship's well-being. Partners can cultivate a deeper connection and a more satisfying and enduring partnership through mutual sacrifice and dedication, finding joy in the fulfillment that comes from prioritizing the relationship.

I like how Rick Warren expounds on life's purpose: "It is not about you. The purpose of your life is far greater than your own personal fulfillment, your peace of mind, or even your happiness."[64] As Powell adds, "Overcoming challenges together as a couple often includes the opportunity to exercise forgiveness, empathy, selfless love, etc. It is as if the challenge provides the opportunity for spouses to reflect on their commitment because if the marriage is to work, the situation requires commitment."[65]

In conclusion, a healthy marriage is built on the rock of commitment, emotional well-being, and mutual respect. Preparing yourself before entering this sacred union is crucial; nurturing excitement and love should be ongoing pursuits. Establishing open, honest communication fosters understanding, while realistic expectations help partners navigate the complexities of shared life. Financial planning and spending quality time together further strengthen this bond, allowing couples to cultivate forgiveness and appreciate the role of sacrifice in their relationship.

---

64. Rick Warren, *The Purpose Driven Life: What on Earth Am I Here For?* (Grand Rapids: Zondervan, 2002), 17.

65. Shelly Evans Powell, "Commitment in Marriage: An Influence for Moral Growth" (MS diss., Brigham Young University, 2009), 61, https://scholarsarchive.byu.edu/etd/2225.

It is important to approach marriage with genuine intention and a deep understanding of its principles. Casual attitudes may lead to temporary satisfaction; but without a commitment to the core values of marriage, that satisfaction is likely to fade. By honoring the guidelines inherent in this partnership, couples can avoid turning their union into disunion, ensuring a lasting and fulfilling relationship grounded in unconditional love and mutual growth.

CHAPTER V

SUSTAINING MARITAL COMMITMENT

The ease with which couples can now pursue divorce and the growing acceptance of cohabitation have significantly altered our approach to marriage. This shift has led to a notable decline in traditional institutional marriage and an increase in nontraditional arrangements. As relationships become more focused on personal satisfaction and less on collective growth, the foundational values of marriage seem to be increasingly misunderstood and overlooked. This trend weakens long-term commitment and undermines the stability that marriage once provided.

A thorough grasp of fundamental marital values is crucial for fostering enduring relationships and building a stronger society. Understanding these principles helps form more committed unions and benefits future generations by setting a positive example. As we navigate these changes, we must reflect on and uphold the core values that support lasting partnerships and contribute to a healthier, more cohesive community.

EMBRACING THE JOURNEY
OF LIFELONG COMMITMENT

A marriage will not survive without a commitment through challenges. Embracing the journey of lifelong commitment in marriage requires more than just a promise at the altar; it demands a resolute dedication through every challenge. Marriage is not merely a union of two individuals but a partnership that thrives on mutual commitment, especially during tough times. Couples who face and overcome difficulties together often find that these experiences strengthen their bond, deepen their affection, and foster a sense of selfless love and respect. The ability to navigate challenges successfully hinges on each partner's willingness to set aside personal ego and prioritize the relationship.

Commitment in marriage is fundamentally about focusing on the partnership rather than individual desires. When both partners are dedicated to the union and each other, they create a strong sense of "we-ness," a powerful connection that sustains their relationship through the ups and downs of life. This shared commitment is pivotal for enduring the inevitable hardships of any long-term relationship. The strength of a marriage is built on this mutual dedication, where each partner focuses on supporting and understanding the other rather than solely on their own needs and ambitions.

While the concept of lifetime commitment may be questioned in modern society, it remains a crucial element of a stable and fulfilling marriage. A committed relationship is not just about love but about prioritizing the partnership. It's about teamwork and a shared vision for the future. It's about a deliberate willing to make sacrifices for the sake of the relationship, which in turn strengthens the bond between partners. This dedication transforms marriage from a personal desire into a shared goal in which both individuals are equally invested in nurturing and maintaining their connection.

Research shows the critical role of commitment in sustaining a healthy marriage. Studies reveal that when both partners value their marriage and their roles within it, they report higher levels of commitment. This commitment not only contributes to positive relationship outcomes but also reinforces the stability of the marriage itself. The stability and health of a marital relationship are closely tied to how much importance both partners place on their union, reflecting a broader understanding of marriage as a significant and enduring institution.

The importance of commitment cannot be overstated. It is not just about remaining together but about actively working to strengthen the relationship through mutual respect and shared goals. This ongoing effort ensures that the marriage remains resilient against external pressures and internal conflicts. Couples who prioritize their marriage and their roles within it are more likely to experience a deeper and more fulfilling connection, demonstrating that commitment is critical to a healthy and lasting relationship.

A lasting marriage requires a steadfast commitment that transcends individual desires and focuses on the partnership. By embracing the challenges and maintaining a shared sense of purpose, couples can build a robust and resilient relationship. This dedication enhances their lives and sets a positive example for future generations, reinforcing the enduring value of marriage in a rapidly changing world. Let this reminder of the importance of commitment inspire and motivate you to invest in your relationship.

TRUST SOLIDIFIES COMMITMENT

Trust is a fundamental pillar that solidifies commitment in any relationship. It serves as the bedrock upon which a lasting partnership is built, with couples often basing their commitment on their confidence and faith in each other. However, trust does not develop spontaneously or remain static; it requires deliberate and ongoing effort. Building and maintaining trust involves intentional actions and time, and it is a choice that partners must continually make to invest in one another and their relationship.

While trust forms the foundation of a strong relationship, it is crucial to understand that it cannot be taken for granted. Trust is not a blind reliance but rather a living, dynamic element that needs to be nurtured daily. When partners adopt attitudes or behaviors that erode trust, restoring it to its original level can be challenging. Rebuilding trust takes time and effort; even once restored, it may not return to the same level. Therefore, it is prudent to maintain and value your partner's trust, avoiding actions that could undermine it. Consistently demonstrating reliability and respect through your actions and attitudes helps to keep trust alive and reinforces the strength of the relationship.

As trust deepens, it enhances the emotional connection between partners, providing a deep sense of security and attachment. Consistent, positive interactions lead to a greater sense of attachment and emotional satisfaction, moving beyond mere collaboration to a place where partners genuinely enjoy each other's company. This emotional engagement is a crucial indicator of how dependable and committed each partner is and provide a strong foundation for enduring commitment. When both partners feel emotionally secure and valued, they are likelier to maintain a lasting and fulfilling connection.

When trust is broken due to behavioral or action-related issues, it is possible to rebuild it, provided both partners are committed to the relationship. Rebuilding trust involves mutual effort and may require seeking external help if necessary. It's important to work together to find ways to address and rectify the issues that caused the breach.

Couples can restore their connection and strengthen their relationship by focusing on rebuilding trust. This process, though challenging, offers a hopeful path to a stronger, more resilient relationship. Without trust, a relationship struggles to survive and thrive, much like a ship without a rudder. Therefore, prioritizing and repairing trust is fundamental to weathering any storm and ensuring the relationship's long-term viability.

In essence, trust strengthens a relationship and ensures its stability and depth. By proactively working to build and maintain trust, partners create a secure and supportive environment where both feel valued and understood. This ongoing effort transforms the relationship into a meaningful and enduring partnership capable of withstanding challenges and evolving. Commitment to nurturing trust and emotional engagement is crucial for a lasting and satisfying relationship.

Trust is the backbone of a successful marriage; a relationship may struggle to survive without it. Both partners must remain vigilant and proactive in preserving and rebuilding trust to keep their connection strong and resilient. By making trust a central focus, couples can ensure a deeper, more enduring bond that can navigate the complexities of life together.

MEETING EACH OTHER'S FUNDAMENTAL NEEDS

Understanding and meeting each other's fundamental needs is crucial for fostering a strong and lasting commitment in a marital relationship.

This requires an in-depth awareness of what each partner values most and how those values translate into their essential needs. Meeting each other's profound needs results in engaged commitment and marital satisfaction. Try to understand your spouse's needs and meet those you can meet. For example, women typically prioritize affection, meaningful conversations, and family commitment. Conversely, men often prefer respect, admiration of their efforts, recreational companionship, and sexual fulfillment.

Effective communication is the cornerstone of this process. Married couples should communicate openly and honestly about their desires, expectations, and feelings. For instance, you should express your need for more quality time together or validate a partner's feelings during a disagreement. This involves expressing one's own needs and actively listening to and validating the needs of the other, making them feel heard and understood.

Through regular and meaningful conversations, partners gain a deeper understanding of each other's core values, which helps to foster emotional and psychological well-being. As couples grow in knowledge about each other's thoughts, values, experiences, and future aspirations, they create a stronger emotional connection and intimacy.

Emotional support is another critical component of couples' needs. Each partner needs to feel supported, particularly during stressful times. This support can take many forms, such as reassurance, empathy, and presence. Reassurance involves verbal or non-verbal expressions of confidence and encouragement. Empathy is about sharing your partner's feelings and is a powerful source of emotional support. Presence refers to being there for your partner physically and emotionally. Understanding how each partner prefers to receive support—whether through words of affirmation, acts of service, or quality time—helps to enhance emotional intimacy and ensures that both partners feel cared for in a way that resonates with them.

Mutual respect is integral to maintaining a healthy relationship. Respecting each other's values, interests, and boundaries is crucial for avoiding conflicts and fostering a positive partnership. This means acknowledging and honoring differences without judgment, ensuring both partners feel valued and understood. Respect reinforces commitment and builds a solid foundation for long-term satisfaction. Couples can create a secure and harmonious relationship by prioritizing mutual respect without conflicts and misunderstandings.

Aligning with shared goals and values is vital for creating a unified direction in the relationship. Discussing primary life goals, such as career aspirations, family planning, and personal growth, helps both partners work towards a common vision. For instance, a shared goal of financial stability can lead to discussions about budgeting and saving. A shared value of honesty can lead to open and honest communication. This alignment prevents conflicts and fosters a sense of partnership and mutual purpose. When partners are on the same page, they are more likely to feel connected and committed to their shared future.

Balancing intimacy with independence is relevant for a thriving relationship. While togetherness is important, allowing space for individual growth and interests is equally crucial. This means supporting each other's personal pursuits and respecting each other's need for independence. For instance, you should encourage your partner to pursue their hobbies or career goals while spending quality time together. It's finding a healthy balance where both partners feel supported in their individual growth and connected in the relationship. This balance helps partners grow individually while maintaining a strong connection.

Compromise and flexibility are necessary for resolving conflicts and maintaining harmony. Understanding that each partner may have different needs and being willing to find a middle ground can help address issues effectively. Flexibility in adjusting expectations and being open to change is key to sustaining a balanced and harmonious relationship.

Spending quality time together strengthens the connection between partners. This time should focus on meaningful interactions and shared experiences rather than coexisting. Participating in activities that both partners love and creating memorable moments together fosters a more profound bond and solidifies the overall quality of the relationship.

Physical affection and intimacy are also vital to meeting fundamental needs. Constantly expressions of love, such as hugs, kisses, and intimate moments, contribute to both emotional and physical satisfaction. These acts of affection strengthen the emotional connection and maintain a sense of closeness.

Encouraging each other's personal growth and aspirations is crucial for a fulfilling relationship. Supporting each other's development shows a commitment to individual happiness and well-being, which in turn benefits the relationship as a whole. Making intentional sacrifices to empower your spouse helps extend their potential and reinforces the relationship's foundation.

If you want to empower your spouse to extend their potential, allow yourself to make intentional sacrifices. As Gray declares, "A man is most often hurt, offended, or drained when a woman does not trust, appreciate, or accept his motives, abilities, thinking, decisions, and behavior…. A woman primarily needs to be cared for, understood, and respected. She is the most vulnerable to feeling hurt when her feelings are not respected, understood, or cared for."[66]

---

66. John Gray, *Men, Women, and Relationships* (New York: Harper Paperbacks, 1993), 267.

Understanding and meeting each other's fundamental needs is crucial for a long-lasting marriage. Effective communication is indispensable for expressing and validating needs, while emotional support through empathy and reassurance strengthens the bond. Mutual respect, values, and boundaries reinforce commitment, and aligning on shared goals ensures a unified direction.

Balancing intimacy with personal growth, practicing compromise, and spending quality time together enhance the relationship. Regular physical affection and supporting each other's growth further solidify the partnership. Couples build a resilient relationship capable of enduring challenges and deepening their connection by focusing on these areas.

SPIRITUALITY HELPS WITH MARRIAGE COMMITMENT

Spirituality plays a substantial role in enhancing marital commitment. In the context of marriage, spirituality refers to a shared belief system or a sense of purpose that transcends the individual, in our context, belief in the Lord Jesus Christ. A marriage where both spouses believe in God, pray together, worship together, and minister together usually helps couples navigate challenges more easily, settle conflicts better, forgive more effortlessly, and care more as they have this sense of purpose together. This shared spirituality is a source of strength during difficult times, making the couple more resilient and capable of enduring challenges.

Spirituality can significantly enhance marital commitment by providing a shared sense of purpose, a framework for resolving conflicts, and a source of strength during challenges. For example, shared spiritual beliefs can provide common ground for resolving conflicts, such as turning to prayer for guidance. It can also offer a sense of comfort and strength during difficult times, as couples can draw on their faith for support.

Furthermore, spiritual teachings offer guidance on conflict resolution by emphasizing forgiveness, patience, and understanding. Couples who practice these principles may find it easier to navigate disagreements and reach satisfactory resolutions. The spiritual emphasis on forgiveness and healing encourages couples to release negative emotions, rebuild trust, and strengthen their bond.

Sharing spiritual activities, like attending church services or Bible study groups, reinforces mutual support and connection. This leads to increased empathy, compassion, and stress reduction, all contributing to a more supportive and fulfilling relationship. A shared spiritual commitment also enhances marital dedication, encouraging couples to uphold their vows and work through difficulties with greater resolve.

Research indicates that religiosity serves as a supportive force within relationships, contributing positively to both the stability and quality of the marriage. It also impacts the physical and psychological well-being of the couple and their broader family. By fostering a shared spiritual framework, couples are more likely to experience greater marital satisfaction and commitment while also experiencing reduced levels of conflict and adversity. As Lakatos and Martos argue, "In a positive context, religiosity plays a supportive role in relationships, and has a positive effect on the stability and quality of the relationship, as well as on the physical and psychological well-being of the couple and other family members. Religiosity can influence marital satisfaction, stability, and commitment positively and decrease heightened conflicts and struggles."[67]

---

67. Csilla Lakatos and Tamás Martos, "The Role of Religiosity in Intimate Relationships," *European Journal of Mental Health* 14, no. 2 (2019): 260–279, https://doi.org/10.5708/EJMH.14.2019.2.3.

There is a strong connection between spirituality and marital health. Spiritual involvement often correlates with greater marital satisfaction, lower divorce rates, reduced conflict, and heightened commitment. Couples who adhere to religious practices tend to view divorce as less acceptable and exhibit a greater willingness to make sacrifices for each other, fostering a robust sense of unity. Overall, religiosity significantly enhances marital satisfaction, stability, and commitment while diminishing conflicts and challenges, providing a sense of security and stability in the relationship.

ELIMINATE COMPLACENCY

Complacency in marriage is a significant threat to a relationship's stability and commitment. As time passes, couples may slip into routines that create a misleading sense of security, decreasing effort and engagement. Recognizing where stagnation might occur is crucial in combating this issue. Actively working to keep the relationship vibrant involves not taking each other for granted, engaging in enjoyable activities, exchanging thoughtful gestures, and consistently expressing appreciation. Regularly sharing experiences, such as vacations or simple daily moments, can help maintain a dynamic and fulfilling relationship.

Treat each other with the same care and attention as you did during your first date to counteract complacency. Aim to make each day memorable and enjoyable, even amidst the realities of life—whether it's managing work, children, or other commitments. While maintaining the initial excitement may be challenging, striving to keep the relationship healthy and lively is important. This doesn't mean every interaction needs to be highly romantic or emotional. Instead, focus on demonstrating your effort and commitment through everyday actions.

Being creative in your relationship doesn't require grand gestures or financial expenditure. You can find ways to nurture your connection even while dealing with the busyness of daily life. Simple activities like cooking together, playing games, or sharing meals can foster intimacy and strengthen your bond. The key is to find joy in these moments and appreciate each other's presence and contributions.

Ultimately, the goal is to avoid taking each other for granted and continuously invest in the relationship. Writing your marriage story together involves showing ongoing care and affection and making an effort to keep the relationship exceptional and engaging. By embracing these practices, you ensure that your marriage remains dynamic and fulfilling, reinforcing your commitment to one another. This continuous investment is not just a choice but a necessity for a vibrant relationship. As Bosch et al. insist, "Marriage is not an answer, it is a search. It is a relationship within which change is generated by relating and living together. It can produce growth, identity, and a sense of togetherness. Nurture and strengthen your relationship for lifetime commitment."[68]

Marriage is a continuous journey rather than a final destination; it thrives on the dynamic process of growing and evolving together. This ongoing effort can lead to personal growth, a strengthened identity, and a deeper connection. To sustain a lifetime commitment, couples must avoid complacency, which can lead to neglect and weakening the relationship.

Showing commitment during stable times involves proactively preparing for challenges and fortifying the marriage. This includes resisting the drift into a routine and actively maintaining the sense

---

68. Kathy Bosch, Marilyn Fox, and Gail Brand, "Strengthening the Couple Relationship," *University of Nebraska*, May 2007, https://extensionpublications.unl.edu/assets/pdf/g1716.pdf.

of novelty and excitement that initially fueled the relationship. In essence, protecting your commitment means keeping the initial reasons for your bond vibrant and alive.

REFRAIN FROM HARMING YOUR PARTNER INTENTIONALLY

Refraining from intentionally harming your partner is necessary for maintaining a healthy marriage. Harmful actions, whether overtly aggressive or subtly damaging, can undermine the trust and commitment crucial for a strong relationship. Recognizing behaviors that can inflict harm, such as derogatory comments, belittling your partner's opinions, or engaging in sarcasm and mockery, is important. Even seemingly minor actions, like reckless remarks or thoughtless behavior, can accumulate over time and create lasting damage to your relationship.

Recognizing what constitutes harmful behavior is the pivotal first step in preventing it. Actions like put-downs, neglect, and negative interpretations can gradually erode your partner's self-esteem and emotional well-being. This recognition is crucial for fostering a more supportive and respectful relationship, as it involves being mindful of how your words and actions affect your partner and striving to create a positive environment where both partners feel valued.

Guarding against impulsive actions is also important. Impulsive behaviors, such as making hurtful comments or acting without considering your partner's feelings, can cause lasting damage. It's vital to pause and reflect before reacting, especially during moments of frustration or anger. This mindfulness helps prevent unnecessary harm and maintains a more thoughtful and respectful interaction.

Abusive behavior, whether physical, emotional, or verbal, is profoundly damaging and unacceptable. Committing to non-abusive behavior and seeking help if needed is required for maintaining a safe and loving environment. Similarly, addressing and healing from betrayals—such as affairs or addictions—requires a significant commitment from both partners. Rebuilding trust involves working through the issues, seeking forgiveness, and actively rebuilding the relationship.

In essence, refraining from intentional harm involves consciously acting with kindness, respect, and empathy toward one's partner. By understanding and avoiding harmful behaviors and remaining committed to addressing and overcoming challenges together, couples can protect and strengthen their marital commitment. This proactive stance ensures that the relationship remains a source of support, love, and fulfillment despite the inevitable difficulties. Markman et al. assert, "Many things we do can cause minor or major hurts: putdowns, avoidance, negative interpretations, abusive comments, forgetting something important, making decisions without regard for the needs of our partner, affairs, addictions, impoliteness, and so on."[69]

The commitment to each other may weaken or cease when we do not take a solid stand against the kinds of attacks that come after it. No matter how great the enemy of commitment can be—frustrations, cooling off of sparkle, disappointments, hurt, dissatisfactions, financial challenges, childlessness, children, sickness, if each spouse is mutually determined to stand their ground, their marriage will remain healthy and fulfilling. Gottman and Silver allege that, "In the strongest marriages, husband and wife share a deep sense of meaning. They don't just 'get along'—they also support each other's hopes and aspirations and build a sense of purpose into their lives together." [70]

---

69. Markman, Stanley, and Blumberg, *Fighting for Your Marriage*, 343.

70. Gottman and Silver, Seven Principles for Making Marriage Work, 24.

Refraining from intentional harm involves consciously acting with kindness, respect, and empathy toward your partner. You can protect and strengthen your marital commitment by understanding and avoiding harmful behaviors, practicing effective communication, and addressing each other's needs. This proactive approach ensures that your relationship remains a source of support, love, and fulfillment, even in the face of inevitable challenges.

DEVELOP A SELFLESS ATTITUDE

Developing a selfless attitude is crucial for building and maintaining a thriving marriage. Selflessness means putting your partner's needs and well-being ahead of your own desires and interests. In contrast, self-centeredness, often glorified in modern culture, can undermine relationship satisfaction and stability. Partners prioritizing each other's needs and well-being creates a foundation of genuine connection and support.

Today, many relationships are influenced by self-serving motives. Questions like, What do I gain from this relationship? Can my partner provide financial or emotional stability? Is my partner financially or professionally stable? Will they provide for me throughout my life? Will they handle daily chores like cooking and cleaning? Will they take on childcare responsibilities while I do little? Will they support my extended family and protect me? often shape people's views on marriage. While it's important to consider practical aspects such as financial stability and shared responsibilities, these should not be the primary reasons for entering into a marriage. If your relationship is based solely on these factors, it lacks the depth needed to weather the storms of life.

A marriage built on self-serving motives is like a house built on sand—its stability is precarious. The relationship may falter when the initial reasons that drew you to your partner fade or change. Genuine marital commitment comes from enduring love and mutual respect, not a desire for personal gain. When the foundation of a relationship is grounded in self-centered interests, it is vulnerable to collapse when faced with life's inevitable challenges.

Choosing a partner based on their current status, wealth, or career can be misguided. These aspects of a person's life are subject to change. Careers evolve, wealth can fluctuate, and status can shift. However, a commitment based on genuine love and a desire to support each other through life's ups and downs will endure. A relationship founded on genuine affection and mutual support is more resilient and better equipped to handle the inevitable changes that come with time.

For instance, if your marriage is built on superficial or self-serving reasons such as financial security or social status, it's careful to reassess your perspective. Reflect on your motives and consider changing to foster a more selfless and loving approach. It's never too late to shift your mindset and realign your priorities. Focusing on genuine love and mutual support can give your marriage true happiness.

A selfless attitude transforms a relationship from a transactional arrangement into a deep, meaningful partnership. It takes understanding, effort, and a willingness to prioritize your partner's needs and happiness. By embracing selflessness and nurturing a genuine connection, you create a marriage that survives and thrives through all life's challenges. Your commitment to making your relationship a happy and fulfilling space will bring you and your spouse lasting joy and satisfaction, inspiring and motivating couples to adopt a selfless attitude.

Developing a selfless attitude is fundamental to a successful marriage. It involves prioritizing your partner's needs over personal gain and fostering a deep, meaningful connection based on genuine love and respect. By shifting away from self-serving motives and focusing on mutual support and understanding, you lay the groundwork for a resilient and fulfilling relationship. Embrace this approach to build a strong marriage that brings lasting happiness.

AVOID EXCUSES, BLAME, AND IRRESPONSIBILITY

Making excuses, assigning blame, and avoiding responsibility can significantly undermine your commitment to each other. These behaviors sap the very essence of love and partnership that hold a marriage together. Today, many people have developed a habit of shifting blame and dodging accountability. This tendency creates a cycle of excuses and finger-pointing, deepening problems without offering real solutions. In a marriage, this pattern can be especially detrimental, leading to a breakdown in communication and trust.

When you listen to couples who are constantly at odds, a common theme emerges: both partners blame each other for the state of their relationship. Each person avoids taking responsibility for their actions and instead focuses on the faults of the other. This cycle of blame and excuse-making prevents any real progress and keeps the relationship from moving forward. Without addressing individual contributions to the problems, the relationship is likely to stagnate or even deteriorate.

Reflecting on your attitude, behavior, and actions is crucial to breaking this cycle. Take an honest look at what you might have done to contribute to the issues in your relationship. Once you identify your mistakes, openly discuss them with your partner. Share what you've learned from your missteps and outline your plan for addressing the problem. Your partner should be encouraged to do the same.

This mutual accountability can pave the way for resolving conflicts and improving your relationship rather than allowing issues to fester and grow.

Excuses also play a destructive role in relationships. For instance, if one partner excels in certain areas and the other doesn't, it can lead to resentment and manipulation. A skilled partner in one area might use that skill to coerce the other into taking on more responsibilities or fulfilling specific roles. This kind of behavior creates an imbalance and undermines the partnership. Recognize and appreciate each other's strengths and weaknesses, and work together to find a fair distribution of responsibilities.

Everyone has flaws that can impact their marriage. What matters most is recognizing these flaws, taking responsibility for them, and working together to build a healthier relationship. Blaming your spouse or making excuses only perpetuates problems and prevents growth. Instead, focus on constructive changes and address issues directly. By doing so, you can strengthen your marriage. As the Kendricks state, "Love doesn't pass the blame so easily or justify selfish motives… Love doesn't make excuses. Love keeps working to make a difference in you and in your marriage…Love is responsible and is willing to admit and correct its faults and errors up front."[71]

Avoiding excuses and blame is weighty for a healthy and thriving marriage. It requires taking personal responsibility, recognizing and addressing your own contributions to problems, and working collaboratively with your partner to find solutions. This approach resolves conflicts and builds a stronger foundation of trust and respect. Moving away from blame and excuses can foster a more loving and resilient relationship.

---

71. Stephen and Alex Kendrick, *The Love Dare* (Nashville: B & H Publishing Group, 2008), 127.

PRACTICING HONESTY INFUSED WITH LOVE, EMPATHY, RESPECT, AND CONSIDERATION

Practicing honesty within the framework of love, empathy, respect, and consideration is crucial for nurturing healthy relationships and fostering genuine commitment in marriage. It is not merely enough to tell the truth when necessary; it is reasonable to master the art of conveying that truth. This means being honest in a way that is considerate of your partner's feelings, empathetic to their perspective, and respectful of their dignity. This nuanced approach ensures that honesty enhances rather than undermines the connection between partners.

How truth is communicated can significantly impact its reception. Truth told in a demeaning, insulting, or disrespectful way can inflict deep emotional wounds and strain the relationship. Conversely, truth delivered with respect, kindness, and empathy can heal and strengthen bonds. The key lies in expressing the truth—whether with patience, care, love, or with disdain and contempt. Mastering this art is fundamental for maintaining a healthy and supportive relationship.

In marriage, the principles of respectful communication are even more critical. Your spouse is not just another person in your life; he or she is your partner, deserving of the highest level of respect and consideration. The tone, delivery, and attitude with which you share your truths matter greatly. Ensuring that your communication reflects love and respect mitigates misunderstandings and fosters a deeper, more resilient connection.

When addressing issues within the relationship, the intention behind sharing the truth should be to resolve conflicts and address problems constructively. Truth shared with love, respect, and empathy aims to solve issues rather than exacerbate them. This approach addresses the immediate problem and reinforces the trust and commitment between partners.

Individuals who communicate truth with respect and compassion earn genuine respect, loyalty, and affection from others. Such a communication style enhances relationships and fosters an environment where both partners feel valued and understood. It is a practical approach that leads to healthier, more supportive interactions.

If you struggle with conveying the truth, consider how you would like to receive it. Strive to emulate the respect and care you wish to be shown. Failure to communicate truth with kindness and consideration can deteriorate the relationship, causing harm that may be difficult to repair.

Building and maintaining positive and supportive relationships ultimately depends on how truth is communicated. Approaching truth-telling with empathy and respect can transform challenges into opportunities for growth, ensuring that your relationship remains strong and resilient. Embrace this approach, and you will likely find that your relationships become more meaningful and enduring.

IMPROVE MARRIAGE JOY AND INTIMACY BY ACTS OF KINDNESS

Small acts of kindness can significantly enhance joy and intimacy in marriage. Often, we underestimate the profound impact of these seemingly minor gestures. Actions such as taking on household chores, bringing home small gifts, or leaving thoughtful notes can hold immense meaning for our spouses. Simple acts like offering a positive comment after completing tasks—taking out the garbage, collecting the mail, or cooking dinner—can significantly strengthen the connection between partners. Additionally, dressing nicely, showing understanding, being open to compromise, and standing by each other through life's challenges all contribute to a deeper, more supportive relationship.

Acts of kindness extend beyond daily chores and responsibilities. They also include small, spontaneous gestures of thoughtfulness, such as putting the kids to bed or offering a comforting word when your spouse has had a rough day. Expressing appreciation for your spouse's efforts and acknowledging their contributions, even when things aren't perfect, reinforces your commitment to each other. Supporting each other's friends and family members through emotional support or practical help further demonstrates your dedication to maintaining a solid partnership.

Despite their seemingly insignificant nature, acts of kindness wield a transformative power in marriage. When executed sincerely and periodically, they forge a stronger bond between partners. These gestures, born out of genuine care and concern, are the bedrock of a healthy, enduring relationship. Over time, these seemingly small acts amass, creating a foundation of trust and affection that can stand against the test of time and trials.

If you are hesitant to engage in these gestures, initiating change is worth the effort. You might be surprised by how pleasantly these actions can impact your relationship. Investing time and effort in caring for your partner through intentional, small acts of kindness can lead to a more fulfilling and connected marriage.

Ultimately, the key to enhancing marital joy and intimacy lies in the consistent practice of these small gestures. While they may seem insignificant individually, their cumulative effect can profoundly improve your relationship. By consciously incorporating periodic acts of kindness, you contribute to a deeper and more satisfying connection with your spouse.

Nurturing your marriage through small acts of kindness is a duty and a source of immense joy and satisfaction. Whether it's daily chores, thoughtful comments, or spontaneous gestures, these actions are a testament to your care and reinforce the bond between partners. Embracing and practicing these gestures will improve your relationship and foster a more supportive and loving partnership, inspiring you to continue this journey.

RESPONSIBLE PARENTING AND REINFORCED MARITAL COMMITMENT

Children can cause parents to divorce because parenting styles may sometimes clash and wound your commitment to each other. Responsible parenting significantly reinforces marital commitment, which is essential in fostering a healthy and functional family unit. Parents often find that differences in parenting styles can lead to conflict and strain within their relationship.

This discord can ultimately challenge their commitment to each other. By developing a mutual understanding of each parent's role and impact within the family, couples can create a more functional and effective family dynamic. Each partner brings unique life experiences and perspectives to parenting, which can complement each other if acknowledged and respected.

Typically, in many families, one parent tends to be more lenient while the other is firmer and more structured. This balance of "carrots and sticks" is crucial for children's psychological development. Children need both nurturing and discipline to grow into empathetic, resilient adults. Excessive harshness can lead to emotional damage, fostering a lack of empathy and compassion. Conversely, overly permissive parenting can result in a lack of resilience, leading children to struggle with life's challenges. The rise of "gentle parenting" in America, which emphasizes permissiveness over discipline, can lead to children lacking clear moral guidance and accountability, detrimental to societal cohesion in the long run.

Parents must skillfully blend both parenting styles to teach children how to develop strong character traits. The goal is to find a balanced approach that combines discipline with understanding. Achieving this balance requires both parents to acknowledge and respect each other's contributions to their children's upbringing. Disregarding or dismissing a partner's parenting style can undermine their collective effectiveness and negatively impact the children's well-being.

Creating a positive family climate involves numerous factors, such as fostering quality relationships between parents and children, providing incentives, and maintaining open, positive communication. Effective parenting includes understanding each child's needs and offering appropriate guidance and supervision. These elements work together to support children's behavior and development, providing a protective buffer against potential issues.

When parents engage in responsible parenting, it reinforces their commitment to each other. Proactive and supportive parents set a strong example. You can be good leaders in your homes by being role models to your children. You have the opportunity to inspire healthy ethics of integrity, care, forgiveness, love, peace, cohesion, hard work, and respect, teach your children that character matters, and be actively involved in their daily lives. This active involvement helps instill these values in children, making them more likely to develop into well-rounded adults with strong moral compasses. Responsible parenting is a powerful tool that increases your commitment to each other.

Conversely, irresponsible parenting inhibits marital commitment. Behaviors such as lack of involvement, constant conflict, poor conflict resolution, and unhealthy habits like substance abuse, addicted gambling, rigidness, or domestic violence can profoundly affect children's emotional stability. These negative patterns not only harm the children but also weaken the marital bond, creating a detrimental cycle of dysfunction. By being aware of these behaviors and actively working to avoid them, parents can strengthen their commitment to each other and create a healthier family environment.

Investing time and energy into parenting is pressing for nurturing a supportive and protective environment for children. This commitment involves dedicating resources, patience, and effort to guide and support their development. By investing in your children, you become a source of support, protection, refuge, and optimism for them. The rewards of such investment are manifold: strengthened family bonds, increased satisfaction within the family unit, and solidified marital commitment between parents.

Working together in their parenting roles can enhance couples' relationships and build a stronger, more unified family. This joint effort benefits the children and reinforces the marital partnership. When both parents actively participate and support each other in raising their children, it fosters a sense of shared purpose and mutual respect.

Responsible parenting is a foundation for a committed and healthy marriage. It challenges both partners to work collaboratively, acknowledge each other's strengths, and support one another through the trials of raising children. This mutual effort helps raise well-adjusted children and deepens the marital bond, making the family unit more resilient and cohesive.

DIVORCE IMPACTS DIVORCEES
AND THEIR CHILDREN

Understanding the implications of divorce is essential before deciding to end a marriage. Recognizing these effects can provide a clearer perspective on whether to resolve conflicts or pursue separation. While divorce might be a necessary option for individuals facing domestic abuse, repeated infidelity, or neglect, research indicates that the negative consequences often outweigh any potential benefits. Divorce brings significant mental, financial, emotional, and physical repercussions that impact not only the individuals involved but also their children and future generations.

Mentally and emotionally, divorce typically triggers immediate stress and upheaval. The emotional impact can be severe, leading to anxiety, depression, and feelings of failure. Individuals may struggle with self-esteem and experience ongoing sadness or confusion. This emotional strain often clouds judgment, making managing practical aspects such as work responsibilities and co-parenting challenging. Over time, this stress can contribute to chronic health issues, including hypertension and insomnia, with potential long-term effects such as increased risks for cardiovascular diseases and mental health disorders.

Drs. Raley and Sweeney claim that divorce might contribute to decline in well-being because of short-term turmoil surrounding the crisis of marital disruption, and it might also affect long-term health outcomes by depriving individuals of material, psychic, and social resources that derive from marriage. The past decade has produced substantial evidence to support the crisis model, particularly regarding mental health.[72]

---

72. R. Kelly Raley and Megan M. Sweeney, "Divorce, Repartnering, and Stepfamilies: A Decade in Review," *Journal of Marriage and Family* 82, no.1 (2020): 81-99, doi:10.1111/jomf.12651.

Financially, divorce imposes substantial strain. The economic burden of maintaining two separate households can be overwhelming. Divorcees may struggle to meet their financial needs while dealing with child support and legal expenses. This financial strain often results in a lower standard of living and heightened anxiety about future financial stability. Additionally, the stress from divorce can impact job performance, affecting concentration, job satisfaction, and potential career advancement.

Children of divorced parents often face their own sets of challenges. Maintaining emotional connections with their parents can be difficult, and their academic performance may suffer. Frequent transitions between homes can lead to feelings of insecurity and difficulties in establishing consistent relationships. Research suggests that children from divorced families may be at a higher risk for academic struggles and behavioral issues, including lower self-esteem and engagement in risky behaviors.

Divorce's impact can go beyond immediate family and influence future generations. Children from divorced families are more likely to encounter marital difficulties in their own relationships. This pattern can continue into the next generation, with children of divorced individuals potentially experiencing similar issues in their own marriages. The cycle of marital discord and divorce may perpetuate instability and emotional distress across generations. As Paul Amato and Jacob Cheadle contend, "Experiencing parental divorce as a child appears to increase the risk of a variety of problems in adulthood. Compared with adults with continuously married parents, adults with divorced parents tend to obtain less education, earn less income, have more troubled marriages, have weaker ties with parents, and report more symptoms of psychological distress."[73]

---

73. Paul R. Amato and Jacob Cheadle, "The Long Reach of Divorce: Divorce and Child Well-Being across Three Generations," *Journal of Marriage and Family* 67, no.1 (2005): 191-206, doi:10.1111/j.0022-2445.2005.00014.x.

Understanding the broad implications of divorce highlights the importance of addressing marital issues proactively. Recognizing the significant mental, financial, emotional, and physical consequences can encourage couples to seek counseling or other forms of support before making such a drastic decision. Though divorce can be a positive thing in certain situations, it can lead to immediate turmoil and long-term declines in well-being, affecting various aspects of life and future generations.

In conclusion, in happy and fulfilling marriages, partners remain steadfastly committed to their vows, regardless of their challenges. This genuine commitment entails uplifting each other, forging a shared sense of purpose, celebrating small and significant achievements, maintaining a deep friendship, showing mutual respect, taking ownership of responsibilities, engaging in honest communication, and selflessly caring for one another. At the heart of relationships lies commitment, and active commitment fosters a marriage's longevity.

There is unparalleled joy in traversing life's journey with a partner who stands by you unconditionally, comprehends you, shields and cherishes you, fulfills your needs, and prioritizes your interests above their own. As Markman et al. conclude, "There is virtually nothing you can do that has more power to enhance your life than to build and protect a great and happy marriage. It's also one of the best things you can possibly do to enhance your children's well- being."[74]

---

74. Markman, Stanley, and Blumberg, *Fighting for Your Marriage*, 68.

CHAPTER VI

MASTERING EFFECTIVE COMMUNICATION

Communication is an indispensable skill that everyone must strive to enhance at various points in life. It transcends mere words and is an ongoing competence that evolves over time. Even experts in communication acknowledge its intricacies and challenges. Indeed, communication ranks among the foremost hurdles in marital relationships. Therefore, acquiring knowledge on effective communication with your spouse is crucial. Marriages often become battlegrounds where conflict becomes the norm due to ineffective communication.

Conflict arises when couples neglect to learn effective communication strategies, opting instead to avoid difficult conversations that can escalate into detrimental issues later on. Couples who fail to establish effective communication methods may find maintaining a happy marital life challenging.

Research has proven marital interventions are limited, or sometimes unproductive, in improving marital satisfaction clinically. In fact, some structured marital therapies, and particularly communi-cation skills training in the context of such interventions, have come under fire. Research on marital programs suggests that these interven-tions are often unsuccessful in altering marital satisfaction in clinically significant ways. A comprehensive meta-analysis of published and unpublished couples therapy outcome studies concluded that approx-imately one-third of marital treatment couples showed no improve-ment, and even among those couples who did improve, many still remained within the distressed range on marital satisfaction scales.[75]

Communication sets the foundation for positive influence on other areas of the marriage, so when there are major issues with communica-tion, other areas of the marriage could be affected.[76] That is why mar-ried couples need to learn practical communication skills to improve marital satisfaction and lower the frequency and degree of conflicts.

As previously mentioned, couples require assistance in commu-nicating meaningfully and efficiently. One contributing factor is the inherent differences between men and women in their thought pro-cesses, actions, comprehension, reactions, perceptions, and analyses. Therefore, it is necessary to acquire the skills necessary for effective communication. Within marriage, love encompasses its own unique communication style.

Familiarizing yourself with communication style can enhance mutual understanding between you and your spouse, facilitate con-flict resolution, reduce misunderstandings, boost self-esteem, clarify misconceptions, and foster a harmonious marriage.

---

75. W. R. Shadish et al., "Effects of Family and Marital Psychotherapies: A Meta-analysis," *Journal of Consulting and Clinical Psychology* 61, no.6 (1993): 992-1002, https://doi.org/10.1037/0022 -006X.61.6.992.

76. Williamson, "The Biblical Model of Marriage in Preventing Divorce."

In this chapter, we will explore constructive communication techniques, barriers to genuine communication, and ways spouses can enhance communication effectiveness to reduce conflicts, misunderstandings, and marital dissatisfaction.

MEN AND WOMEN'S PERSPECTIVES IN COMMUNICATION

Men and women naturally view life from different perspectives. These differences are not deficiencies but rather complementary qualities. Married couples should strive to understand these divergent perspectives. When partners fail to appreciate and adapt to these differences, misunderstandings, and conflicts can arise. While some of these differences are universal, others may be more specific to each individual, making personalized understanding crucial.

Typically, men approach situations with a rational mindset, while women tend to infuse their perspectives with emotional considerations. This doesn't mean these tendencies are set in stone or don't fluctuate. However, men are often more inclined toward logical reasoning, whereas women may prioritize emotional aspects in their approach. Each partner must acknowledge and empathize with the other's approach for effective conflict resolution. Recognizing that your spouse's perspective is valid, even if it differs from yours, is fundamental for constructive communication.

Moreover, men often think about the future and plan ahead, while women might focus more on the present moment and immediate experiences. This difference in orientation can influence how each partner handles various aspects of life and decision-making. Men might be more inclined to discuss long-term goals, while women may prioritize current feelings and immediate concerns. Understanding this dynamic can help partners navigate discussions and decisions more harmoniously.

Another key difference is in the way respect and affection are valued. Men typically appreciate respect and acknowledgment of their leadership roles, while women place a high value on emotional affection and reassurance. When women offer their perspectives, it is beneficial to do so in a manner that respects their partner's position as a leader. Similarly, men should recognize that women value and need emotional connection and support. Developing a balance between these needs is crucial for a healthy relationship.

For women, allowing their partners to take the lead and respecting their role can lead to a deeper connection and appreciation. When men feel secure in their position and valued for their contributions, they are more likely to reciprocate with profound affection and care. This mutual respect and understanding create a foundation for a loving and enduring relationship.

Men often have interests and hobbies, such as outdoor activities or sports, and enjoy spending time with friends. It's important for women to support these interests rather than discourage them. For instance, if your husband enjoys playing golf, you can encourage him to join a local club or plan a weekend getaway for a golfing trip. Allowing men the freedom to pursue their passions benefits their well-being and strengthens the relationship. Trying to inhibit their interests can lead to frustration and resentment, so giving space for individual pursuits can benefit both partners.

It's important to note that these observations are based on general trends and may not apply universally. Individuals vary greatly; some men and women may exhibit traits contrary to these generalizations. However, understanding these fundamental differences can foster better communication and mutual understanding. Being open to these differences helps in navigating relationship dynamics more effectively.

Everett Worthington, Jr. suggests six steps to communicating better:

- Identify the difficulties.
- Do not try to change everything at once.
- Begin with the positive.
- Analyze the situations carefully.
- Do not lose sight of the goal: to communicate valuing love in a positive way.
- Get a book that described a structured way to change communication.[77]

Ultimately, successful communication in a marriage involves both partners expressing their viewpoints respectfully and being receptive to each other's perspectives. The ongoing process of learning from one another and growing together is invaluable. Embracing each other's unique perspectives enriches the relationship and fosters a deeper connection. Don't shy away from exploring and understanding your spouse's viewpoint—good communication is the cornerstone of strong relationships and fulfilling marriages.

CELEBRATE DIFFERENCES AS COMPLEMENTARY

Embracing and celebrating partners' differences can transform obstacles into opportunities for growth and improved communication.

---

77. Everett L. Worthington, Jr., *Hope-Focused Marriage Counseling: A Guide to Brief Therapy* (IVP Academic / Intervarsity Press: Downers Grove, 2005), 157.

Instead of viewing these differences as threats to your freedom, happiness, or peace, recognize them as unique contributions that enrich your relationship. Each person brings distinct qualities and perspectives to the table, which, when appreciated, can enhance your connection and personal growth. Treating differences as liabilities or weaknesses only creates barriers, while celebrating them fosters a more harmonious and supportive partnership.

It is crucial to understand that significant aspects of your partner's character and attitudes are unlikely to change dramatically. No matter how committed you are to altering these traits, focusing on changing your partner can be fruitless. Instead, invest your energy in accepting and adapting to who your spouse is. This acceptance is not about resigning yourself to dissatisfaction but about aligning your expectations with reality and learning to appreciate your partner's inherent qualities.

Differences naturally create friction, impacting various aspects of your partner's worldview, beliefs, attitudes, emotions, and actions. This friction isn't necessarily negative; it can catalyze personal and relational growth. By approaching these differences with an open mind, you can use them to understand each other better. Rather than resisting change, view it as a chance to evolve together and become better versions of yourselves.

Life would indeed be monotonous if everyone were the same. The foundation of a healthy relationship lies in the dynamic interplay of diverse perspectives and experiences. Most people resist change and prefer to remain within their comfort zones. However, genuine growth and meaningful connections come from stepping outside those zones and being open to influence. Flexibility and mutual influence are key to fostering a relationship where communication and understanding flourish.

One effective way to bridge the gap created by differences is through empathetic communication. Putting yourself in your partner's shoes and genuinely trying to understand their perspective can significantly improve how you relate to each other. Empathy allows you to see beyond your viewpoint and appreciate the richness your partner's differences bring to the relationship. It helps resolve conflicts and build a stronger, more resilient partnership.

As Leigh and Clark claim, "Empathy means understanding a person's perspective by putting oneself in his or her shoes. Many researchers have shown that empathy is important for relationship satisfaction. People are more likely to feel good about their marriage and spouse if their partner expresses empathy towards them."[78]

One meaningful way to honor the differences between you and your spouse is by focusing on changing yourself before asking them to do the same. If change were as simple as it sounds, you'd start with yourself rather than trying to impose it on your partner. Just like how Jesus calls us to grow and transform into more compassionate versions of ourselves—a process that unfolds gradually and requires patience—personal change is never immediate or easy. By demonstrating a genuine commitment to bettering yourself, you set an example that can inspire your spouse also to put in the effort to evolve. This process is challenging and requires courage, dedication, and hard work.

It's important to recognize that the changes you hope for in your spouse might sometimes be unrealistic or even unfair. While there are behaviors that need to be addressed, it's crucial to approach these changes with grace and understanding. Supporting each other through growth—without condoning negative behavior—can benefit your relationship more than trying to force immediate change. Ultimately,

---

78. Leigh and Clark, "Human Relations."

it would be best to adopt strategies that suit both you and your spouse, remembering that mutual respect and patience will go a long way in nurturing a healthy, supportive partnership.

Celebrating and embracing differences within a marriage can flip potential conflicts into opportunities for growth and enrichment. Accepting that some aspects of your partner will remain constant allows you to focus on adapting and appreciating these traits. The friction of differing perspectives can lead to personal development and a deeper connection. By stepping out of your comfort zones and approaching each other empathetically, you create a more dynamic and fulfilling relationship. Embrace these differences as complementary elements that contribute to a stronger, more vibrant partnership.

IDENTIFY THE MESSAGE
YOU NEED TO CONVEY

How can you communicate meaning or understanding to your spouse if you cannot identify the message you intend to convey? The first step to effective communication is self-assessment and disclosure—taking the time to reflect on your thoughts and feelings so you can express them clearly. Effective communication with your spouse starts with clearly understanding the message you want to convey.

Before you engage in any discussion, it's crucial to reflect on your thoughts and emotions. This self-assessment allows you to clarify what you truly need to express and ensures that your message is both accurate and purposeful. Without this reflective process, you'll likely communicate disorganizedly or unclearly, leading to misunderstandings or even unintentional hurt.

Failing to prepare and clarify your message before initiating a conversation can be detrimental. If you enter a discussion without fully understanding what you want to say, you risk delivering your message poorly or causing additional conflict. It's not about crafting a perfect speech but about having a clear sense of what you wish to communicate. Unfiltered, spontaneous remarks are often less effective and can lead to deeper misunderstandings. Taking time to process your thoughts ensures that your communication is thoughtful and constructive.

Once you've wisely formulated the message, the next vital step is to convey it with sensitivity and respect. Approach the conversation with love, care, and humility, aiming to foster an environment of open and constructive dialogue. This means presenting your thoughts in a manner that acknowledges your spouse's feelings and encourages mutual understanding. Effective communication is as much about how you deliver your message as it is about the content. A respectful and considerate approach helps to bridge gaps and strengthens your relationship.

It's also important to recognize that communication involves speaking and ensuring your spouse is engaged. As Rodney Ashley highlights, we often believe we are communicating effectively simply because we are talking, but this doesn't guarantee that our message is being heard or understood. Just because someone is present physically doesn't mean they are fully attentive or receptive. Being mindful of this can help you adjust your approach to ensure that your partner is genuinely engaged in the conversation.[79]

To communicate effectively with your spouse, start by clearly identifying and understanding the message you want to convey. Prepare your thoughts to avoid misunderstandings and potential conflicts.

---

79. Rodney R. Ashley, "Equipping Church Leaders to Use Intergenerational Gospel Communication Skills" (DIS diss., Faith International University, 2023), 56, https://www.proquest. com/openview/e3c442d044f54b63511cbf525f9a62b8/1?pqorigsite=gscholar&cbl=18750&diss=y.

Deliver your message with care and respect, creating a space for meaningful dialogue. Lastly, ensure that your spouse is fully engaged in the conversation. Doing so builds a stronger, more resilient relationship where both partners feel heard and valued.

Effective communication hinges on clarity, preparation, and respectful delivery. You can nurture a deeper connection and mutual understanding by taking the time to understand and articulate your message thoughtfully and ensuring that your spouse is truly engaged. This approach will enhance the quality of your interactions and contribute to a more harmonious and supportive relationship.

DEVELOPING ACTIVE LISTENING SKILLS TO COMMUNICATE EFFECTIVELY

Effective communication with your spouse involves active listening, which includes listening without interruptions, taking turns to speak, and responding with care and attention. This approach helps convey your message clearly and makes problem-solving a more collaborative and enjoyable experience rather than a stressful one.

Active listening plays a key role in successful communication. Couples often recognize that being a good listener and being honest are key traits of effective communication. Practical strategies include knowing the right time to talk, showing humility, and actively listening. Good communication practices involve being engaged, respectful, and solution-oriented, and while there are other strategies, these form a solid foundation for effective interaction. Despite knowing the importance of communication, many couples struggle with its practical application.

To enhance your listening skills, it is important to ensure you and your partner take turns speaking, focusing on your own feelings rather than trying to read each other's minds. The speaker should be positive and avoid accusations, while the listener should be mindful of their body language, avoiding signs of disapproval like eye rolling or crossed arms. Even when there is disagreement, the listener should strive to understand and respect the speaker's viewpoint.

Good listening involves maintaining comfortable eye contact, showing interest through gestures, and adopting an open posture. Avoid distractions and physical barriers, and let the speaker finish without interruptions. Use assertive statements to express your feelings and needs, and carefully manage your tone and emotions. If necessary, take a break to cool down before addressing an issue. Understanding that men and women may have different needs and expectations in communication can also help, as women might expect a level of emotional insight that men may not naturally provide.

Active listening is more nuanced than it might first appear, with various factors influencing how we engage in conversations. Men and women often process, interpret, and communicate differently, leading to misunderstandings if expectations aren't managed carefully. For instance, men generally prefer a pragmatic approach and value respect in conversations, while women tend to appreciate more affection and emotional support. When faced with a problem, men might feel inclined to find a solution immediately, but sometimes, the best approach is to listen and be present without trying to fix things immediately. On the other hand, women might want to share their feelings and be heard without needing immediate solutions.

Conversely, women should be mindful that men often prefer straightforward communication and can become impatient with excessive details. Men are often solution- oriented, so providing clear, concise information can help them engage more effectively. Women should also focus on one issue at a time during discussions. Bringing up multiple problems or dredging up past grievances can overwhelm and frustrate men, making it harder to address the current issue. Effective communication is about understanding these differences and adapting your approach to each other's needs. By honing these skills, you can foster more productive and empathetic interactions in your relationship.

Aviva Williamson lists tools and ways for effective communication as follows:

> Practical implementation of effective communication skills includes being a great active listener, displaying engagement in the conversation, knowing when to engage in a conversation after a disagreement, speaking in respectful tones, and the willingness to reach solutions. These major aspects of being a great communicator do not negate other necessary strategies to be effective, but they lay a strategic foundation for couples to be taught how to communicate. On a positive note, 80% of couples understand the importance of communication in marriage, although they may not know how to effectively take the task on.[80]

There are multiple strategies for improving your listening skills, a valuable ingredient to a beneficial engagement with your spouse. The State Government of Victoria recommends,

> Listening is a very important part of effective communication. A good listener can encourage their partner to talk openly and honestly.[81]

---

80. Williamson, "The Biblical Model of Marriage in Preventing Divorce."

81. The State Government of Victoria. "Relationships and Communication." Better Health Channel. Last modified December 25, 2024. https://www.betterhealth.vic.gov.au/health/healthyliving/relationships-and-communication.

In addition, Richmond states that because the one listening does not own the problem, he or she has to remain calm enough to hear the problem. The listener does not have to agree, disagree, or debate. The one talking should share thoughts and feelings without accusing, attacking, or labeling. The goal is a deep understanding of a spouse based on the safety of the communications. The problem is that women and men have different levels of need for talk. Women tend to be more intuitive in reading emotions and moods than men, which is sometimes called "emotional intelligence." [82] This leads to the problem of a woman expecting that a man will understand them like a female friend would and are then disappointed when this does not happen. Women are also disappointed when their husbands do not invest sufficient time in intimate talk or give them undivided attention.

FOCUS ON WHAT BENEFITS YOUR MARRIAGE, NOT WHAT IS COMFORTABLE FOR YOU

It would be best to focus on what truly benefits your marriage rather than taking the "easy way out" or seeking immediate comfort. What feels good in the moment isn't always what's best. Often, the best path involves some exploration and effort, but once you commit to it, you'll see the positive changes. It starts with improving your communication style proactively and fruitfully. For example:

1. After a heated argument, try to open up instead of withdrawing and staying silent in your little bubble for days. Acknowledge your part that led to the argument and initiate a meaningful conversation.

---

82. Richmond Laney, "Marriage as a Spiritual Discipline: Principles and Benefits" (DMin diss., Liberty University, May 2014), 62, https://digitalcommons.liberty.edu/doctoral/845.

2. Rather than building defensive walls after a disagreement, seek common ground to reconnect with your partner. Being always defensive will never take you to a safe place where both of you feel communication is effortless and beneficial to your marriage. It only builds a roadblock to a meaningful conversation.

3. Instead of trying to win the argument, emphasize on winning your relationship. Prioritize what's important for both of you because winning an argument is like winning a battle, but not a war, which can sometimes worsen things.

4. Be open and receptive to your partner's perspective, rather than playing the victim or feeling offended in every conflict. Consider their needs and feelings instead of always focusing on yours. Constantly focusing on your own needs will push your partner to utilize desperate measures that harm your relationship's health.

5. Instead of accusing your partner when misunderstandings arise, take a moment to reflect on your own role in the situation. Approach the issue proactively and respectfully. Everyone has a responsibility in every situation.

6. Rather than always turning to family or friends for help, learn to rely on yourselves to navigate marital challenges. Too much outside influence can complicate things further. Opening the door to outside influence and authority can be damaging. You will grow and preserve your marriage if you learn to communicate effectively with your spouse.

7. Instead of letting anger and resentment build up, tackle the underlying issues head-on. Avoid blaming each other; listen and acknowledge your partner's viewpoint. Don't be afraid to face the reality and problems head-on.

8. Instead of shying away from the root causes of conflict, confront them directly. Until you address these issues, they'll keep resurfacing. Every conflict has its root cause from something, and sometimes we avoid touching the real problem and addressing the surface or the effect. Address the root cause instead and make this conversion the one where your relationship wins.

9. Rather than running away when things get tough, listen to your partner and cultivate positive thoughts and attitudes about your marriage. Don't let negativity take hold.

10. Learn to share your true feelings, concerns, and fears instead of avoiding difficult conversations. Work together to find solutions.

Adopting this constructive communication style and problem-solving approach creates an environment where resentment, confusion, and fear don't accumulate, allowing your relationship to thrive.

COMMUNICATE UNDERSTANDING

As I conducted research for my doctorate studies, I asked participants a straightforward question: What are the most significant issues in marriage today? Across the board, everyone pointed to communication as the top concern. They believe mastering communication skills is crucial for building stronger bonds between spouses. Another question I posed was: How can couples foster healthy relationships in their marriage? Every participant stressed the importance of communication competence in strengthening the connection with their spouse.

One key aspect of communication competence is communicating understanding to your partner. If understanding isn't the goal, it's better to avoid communication altogether. The main reason for starting a conversation with your spouse should be to genuinely understand each other's message, perspective, and goals.

In Thich Nhat Hanh's view, communication requires speaking and hearing. Only together can male and female form life, and only when speaking and hearing are seen as equal parts of communication can understanding be formed. Good communication requires the ability to hear as well as the ability to speak. Communication is a transaction during which understanding is shared and developed. The exchange involved in this transaction is listening and speaking: one party listens, another speaks, and then a response reverses the flow. Through this reciprocity, understanding, but not necessarily agreement, is developed. We communicate to be understood and to understand others. If we're talking and no one is listening (maybe not even our own selves), we're not communicating effectively. There are two keys to effective and true communication. The first is deep listening. The second is loving speech. Deep listening and loving speech are the best instruments I know for establishing and restoring communication with others and relieving suffering.[83]

---

83. Thich Nhat Hanh, *The Art of Communicating* (New York: HarperCollins Publishers Inc., 2013), 22.

COMMUNICATE RESPECTFULLY,
EVEN WITH UNMET NEEDS

When couples' basic needs are unmet, they react negatively toward one another. The results are revealed in their way of communicating. Unmet needs often lead to frustration, despair, and anger in relationships. When we enter marriage, we bring a set of expectations for our partner: we envision them behaving in certain ways, fulfilling specific roles, and meeting particular needs.

When these expectations aren't met, resentment can quickly and easily build up. This growing frustration can lead to diminished communication, where our expressions of dissatisfaction become disrespectful and loveless. Over time, this deterioration can turn our interactions bitter and reduce our ability to connect meaningfully.

To maintain a healthy relationship, one must be mindful of each other's fundamental needs—food, shelter, protection, and care. Neglecting these basic requirements undermines the foundation of the relationship. When issues arise, addressing them promptly and respectfully is crucial.

While not all needs can always be fully met, approaching challenges with a service mindset rather than entitlement fosters a more supportive environment. Love and understanding should guide our communication, even when frustrations arise. By prioritizing grace and compassion, we can navigate difficulties without anger overpowering our connection. As Smalley observes in his book *For Better or for Best*:

> One of the great psychiatrists of our time, Dr. Card Menninger, said that when our basic needs are not met, we move in one of two directions. We either withdraw in

'flight' or turn to 'fight.' The woman who takes the 'flight' approach is certainly not escaping her problems. As she runs, she begins to doubt her self-worth. On the other hand, if she takes the 'fight' approach, she may become an unattractive nag to her husband. I believe the ideal marriage evolves when the wife concentrates on meeting her husband's needs and the husband concentrates on meeting his wife's needs. That combination builds the lasting qualities of a giving relationship.[84]

INVOLVE FRIENDS/FAMILY
WISELY DURING CONFLICT

During conflicts, it's wise for couples to carefully consider what they disclose to friends and family, as well as the advice they receive from them. Neglecting this consideration can lead to increased chaos, instability, and worsened situations. Seeking support and guidance during heated conflicts can be beneficial. However, exercising discernment and critical thinking when implementing external advice can prevent potentially disastrous mistakes and safeguard your marriage.

Family and friends can be important sources of support, especially during overheated conflict, but discretion and judgment are crucial. When frustrated and angry, it's easy to overlook the importance of keeping certain matters private and choosing the right people to confide in. People often only hear the parts of the story we choose to share, missing out on important details that can paint a complete picture. This partial view, combined with their natural tendency to

---

84. Smalley, *For the Better or for the Best*, 15.

side with us, can result in counterproductive advice that exacerbates rather than resolves the issues at hand.

It is vital to protect your marriage and work through problems privately rather than exposing them to outsiders. Every marriage faces its own set of challenges, and it's crucial to shield your relationship from unnecessary external scrutiny. Choose your sources of support carefully, opting for those who respect your marriage and understand boundaries. Those who do not respect these boundaries are not true friends. Share wisely and selectively to maintain your spouse's dignity and ensure the resilience of your relationship.

Remember, your privacy is a key component of your relationship's security, and it's okay to set boundaries with those who offer support. As the Kendricks observe, "Not everyone has the material to be a good friend. Not every man you hunt and fish with speaks wisely when it comes to matters of marriage. Not every woman in your lunch group has a good perspective on commitment and priorities. In fact, anyone who undermines your marriage does not deserve to be given the title of 'friend.'"[85]

SEEK EXTERNAL SUPPORT AND PRAY

When seeking assistance from a counselor, therapist, or marriage specialist, full transparency is a must. Withholding important information from these professionals can significantly limit the effectiveness of their guidance and support. Trust is a crucial component in this process, and it develops over time. If you struggle to trust a marriage specialist, it might be best to consider finding a different professional. The value of the help you receive is directly tied to your willingness

---

85. Stephen and Alex Kendrick, *The Love Dare*, 112.

to be open and honest about your situation. Remember, your trust is a powerful tool in this process; and it's okay to seek help elsewhere if you don't feel it's being respected.

If trust is lacking and you can't open up to the specialist, seeking help elsewhere is more productive than wasting your time and resources. Effective diagnosis and assistance depend on understanding the true nature of the issues at hand, which requires full disclosure. While the specialist's role is to help uncover underlying problems, their ability is significantly hindered without clear, honest communication.

In some cases, the issues within a marriage may be so deeply rooted that external help becomes necessary. It's important to share critical details openly to ensure that the assistance provided is thorough and accurate. Trusting these specialists and their methods is a step toward receiving the comprehensive help you need.

For believers in Christ, it's crucial to remember that many marital struggles can be attributed to spiritual challenges. Everything that manifests itself physically first takes place in the spiritual realm. Effective prayer and seeking divine intervention can be powerful tools in addressing and overcoming these difficulties. Before turning to therapists, dedicate time to praying earnestly for your marriage, asking the Lord to protect and heal it. As stated in James 5:16, "The prayer of a righteous person is powerful and effective."

Satan aims to steal, kill, and rob your marriage of its harmony, health, and stability—nothing less. Understanding this is crucial as you build a personal prayer habit and establish a prayer routine with your spouse to safeguard and nurture your marriage. The good news is that knowing who your enemy is (Satan) makes prayer less daunting. Achieving stability demands earnest and consistent prayer; it should be a regular practice, not just something you turn to occasionally when seeking God's help and intervention. Remember, the power of prayer is real and leads to positive changes in your marriage.

Believe that God answers prayers, even if His answers differ from what you expect. You can expect significant changes when you align yourself with God relationally and pray and fast for your marriage. This personal conviction based on experience—prayer, and faith often yield remarkable results. Remember that prayer should never be your last resort for help. Prayer must be part of your daily routine. Without prayer, it can be difficult to make it far in your marriage; actually, it will.

However, there are times when the situation may have become too complex, or additional factors such as infidelity, drug and gambling addictions, or mental health issues may be at play, making professional help necessary. In such cases, seeking advice from a marriage specialist, church elder, or pastor can be incredibly beneficial. While it might be uncomfortable to open up, saving your marriage is worth stepping out of your comfort zone. Being vulnerable and seeking help is a sign of commitment to restoring and strengthening your relationship.

IDENTIFY ROLES AND RESPONSIBILITIES

Identifying and clearly defining roles and responsibilities within a relationship can significantly improve communication between partners. Establishing a routine where each spouse understands their specific duties, whether daily or regularly, helps streamline household management. This clarity reinforces the household dynamics and makes task fulfillment more manageable, reducing the chances of misunderstandings and conflicts. When both partners know their responsibilities and feel accountable for their roles, it leads to smoother interactions and a more harmonious living environment.

Maintaining an organized household and a balanced relationship becomes challenging without a clear strategy for dividing tasks and responsibilities. A lack of structure often leads to confusion and friction as neither partner knows who is responsible for what. Setting up a flexible system where roles can be adjusted based on circumstances—such as taking on additional duties when a partner is unwell or otherwise occupied—prevents chaos and ensures that essential tasks are always covered. Flexibility is critical, allowing partners to adapt to changing needs and life events while keeping the household running smoothly.

Take, for example, a situation where one partner traditionally handles cooking. If this partner becomes pregnant or falls ill, the other partner should step in to help without hesitation. This temporary adjustment ensures that the household functions seamlessly even when life throws unexpected challenges. It's important to note that roles and tasks are not set in stone but should be organized to support your unique family dynamic best. Each couple must determine their own approach based on their specific needs and preferences.

Ultimately, organization and clear roles within your relationship lead to greater satisfaction and less stress. Household chores like cleaning, cooking, and managing finances should be divided in a way that works for both partners. When each person willingly takes on their share of responsibilities, and both partners communicate effectively about their needs and preferences, the overall happiness and efficiency of the household improve. Discuss your strategy openly, adapt it as necessary, and implement it in a way that best suits your relationship.

To this end, Daniel Richard, through research, explains that when it comes to certain activities such as cooking, cleaning, putting kids to bed, negotiating with schools, paying the bills, grocery shopping, maintaining contact with mutual friends, and organizing family outings, the wives were overwhelmingly completing these tasks over their husbands. The husbands ranked high in activities such as home repairs, yard work, driving on trips, negotiating with credit agencies, and leading the family in spiritual life.[86]

In many households, men often embrace roles that align with leadership and provision. Traditionally, men have taken on responsibilities such as being the primary providers for their families, protecting their loved ones, and handling home maintenance tasks. This sense of leadership extends to making significant family decisions, such as managing large expenses and planning major purchases. Many view these roles as a natural inclination and a duty God gives.

When women allow their partners to lead and make significant decisions, it empowers men to excel in these roles and thrive as the heads of their households. Conversely, when women assume these roles or prevent men from fulfilling them, it can lead to a sense of emasculation, affecting how men serve and relate to their families.

Men often find satisfaction in engaging in practical, hands-on tasks. Activities such as mowing the lawn, trimming trees, barbecuing, and other outdoor chores are typically enjoyed by men, reinforcing their roles as providers and caretakers of their homes. In Christian contexts, men are also seen as spiritual leaders responsible for guiding their families in faith and leading them toward a stronger relationship with God. This spiritual leadership is a fundamental aspect of a man's role within the family.

On the other hand, women often excel in roles centered around

---

86. Richard, "Starving Marriage."

caretaking and organization. Managing day-to-day household activities, including cooking, cleaning, and caring for children, typically falls within their purview. Women frequently oversee tasks such as doing laundry, organizing family events, scheduling appointments, and handling school-related activities. Their organizational skills are instrumental in maintaining continuity and order in the household, contributing significantly to family well-being.

Both men and women are crucial in providing emotional support and empowerment within their families. Each partner brings a unique emotional impact to their relationships with each other and their children. For instance, men often provide support during challenging situations, offering strength and resilience. At the same time, women are adept at creating a nurturing environment that makes everyone feel safe, loved, and cared for.

While traditional roles are still prevalent, modern society often blurs and intertwines these responsibilities. Each family's unique dynamics and circumstances may require a more flexible approach to role distribution. It is bright to adapt these roles according to what works best for your family while considering natural tendencies and preferences.

EDUCATION AND LIFE EXPERIENCE AFFECT COMMUNICATION

Education and life experience significantly shape how we communicate with others, especially in close relationships such as marriage. Despite our proficiency and communication education, miscommunication with a spouse is inevitable. This stems from fundamental differences like social background, emotional intelligence, life experiences, social status, culture, and educational level. These

variations lead people to interpret messages differently, often causing misunderstandings.

The impact of language proficiency and educational background
can be particularly pronounced for couples. These differences become
more evident in intercultural and interethnic marriages and among
couples with varying educational levels. For example, couples with
similar academic achievements, such as having master's degrees, often
find it easier to align their interpretations of life's dynamics. On the
other hand, couples with significant educational disparities may perceive and react to life's challenges differently. While these generalizations hold true in many cases, it's important to recognize that people's
experiences can vary widely, and there are exceptions to these patterns.

Life experience, social status, and environmental background also
contribute to potential miscommunication. I'm not suggesting you
avoid marrying someone with different experiences or status, but
rather acknowledge how these differences can influence your interactions. Having been raised in a modest family where resources were
scarce, I've observed that people from wealthier backgrounds often
approach life with different perspectives and priorities. My friends
from affluent families discussed grand plans, whereas my conversations were often centered around immediate survival and practical
concerns. This disparity in life experiences can lead to differing ways
of interpreting and discussing life events.

We often struggle to understand and interpret life through someone else's lens. This tendency can lead to miscommunication, particularly in marriages where partners come from diverse cultural, social,
and environmental backgrounds. Personal experiences and surroundings shape how we speak and interact with others.

Before moving to the U.S., my understanding of many concepts was quite different. Like many who haven't lived abroad, I assumed that everyone living here was successful, wealthy, and thriving. I had no idea that poverty, homelessness, and life struggles existed in the U.S. I was completely wrong. Just like anywhere else, people in the U.S. face poverty, homelessness, and hardship. I was particularly shocked by the number of homeless people in major cities.

I also used to believe that America was entirely defined by skyscrapers, tall buildings, and urban landscapes, largely due to the countless American movies I had watched. These films shaped my perception, leading me to think that the country had no countryside or rural life. However, when I moved to the U.S., I quickly realized how misguided that idea was. My perspective had been limited by what I had seen in movies rather than by the reality of the diverse environments that exist across the country.

Once I adapted to my new environment, I began to comprehend things more accurately. This shift in perspective helped me recognize how others might have misconceptions based on their own limited experiences, such as assuming that Africa is a single country or that all Africans live in primitive conditions.

I had the privilege of serving as one of the interpreters for a U.S. church on a mission trip to Burkina Faso. I met the group at the airport to help them get to their host's home. As soon as they exited the airport, their lead pastor's first question to me was, "Where are the lions, the huts, the cages, the forest, etc.?" He wasn't joking—he was serious. I had to remind him that he was in the country's largest city, and the things he mentioned could only be found in the villages. But his shock didn't end there. When we arrived at their host's house— a luxurious home with swimming pools, sports rooms, and fancy equipment—he was stunned and couldn't believe he was still in Africa.

This experience made me realize how misconceptions can lead to shock, confusion, and even disappointment. These assumptions often stem from one's limited knowledge or prior experiences. Marriage, like any relationship, can be influenced by similar misconceptions. It's easy to become trapped in one's own viewpoint and forget that one's partner may have a very different perspective shaped by their own experiences.

This highlights the importance of taking the time to educate yourself about your partner. It's key for better communication and understanding. As Thomas and McDonagh claim, "Developing a shared language improves our ability to communicate effectively within our working and personal relationships."[87] Recognizing and accepting that miscommunication often arises from differing experiences and cultural backgrounds can foster greater empathy between partners. Understanding these differences shapes how people view the world can help couples navigate their conversations more effectively. By acknowledging the impact of these factors, partners can work towards bridging their communication gaps and meeting each other halfway.

PROBLEM-SOLVE STRATEGICALLY

In marriage, it's common for conflict to arise for various reasons (unmet expectations, disagreement, gender differences, finance, differing parenting style) and to be derived from different sources (job obligation, friends or family influence, misconception, or misinterpretation of an action or spoken words). Here are a few levels of marriage conflict. Knowing them helps face conflict with a better grasp

---

87. J. Thomas and D. McDonagh, "Shared Language: Towards More Effective Communication," *Australas Med J* 6, no.1 2013):46-54. doi: 10.4066/AMJ.2013.1596.

and better strategies. According to Lantz and Snyder, there are five levels of marital conflict: (1) concealed conflict—in which feelings are "kept under wraps;" (2) overt conflict—out in the open with no attempt to deny the problem; (3) chronic conflict—difficulties become recurrent because unresolved; (4) progressive conflict—continued deterioration with new problems added to old ones; and (5) habitual conflict—in which the couple no longer can or will agree and a high degree of tension results in damage to mental health.[88]

Marital conflicts can be approached from various perspectives, each offering unique insights into the nature of disagreements and strategies for improvement. Systemic therapists often view conflicts as struggles over status and control within the relationship. They believe that tensions arise when partners vie for dominance or influence. To improve communication from this perspective, it's beneficial to focus on establishing clear and fair roles and responsibilities within the relationship. Open discussions about each partner's needs and expectations can help balance power dynamics and prevent conflicts from escalating. Regularly checking in with each other about feelings of fairness and respect can also help maintain a healthy balance of power.

Classic psychoanalysts suggest that marital conflicts may stem from unresolved psychological issues or past experiences affecting the current relationship. To address conflicts from this angle, couples should consider engaging in individual or joint therapy to explore and address deeper emotional issues. This might involve understanding and working through past traumas or unresolved feelings that impact current interactions. Improved communication can be achieved by

---

88. Herman A. Lantz and Eloise C. Snyder, *Marriage: An Examination of the Man-Woman Relationship* (New York: John Wiley and Sons, 1962), 278.

being open about emotional triggers and vulnerabilities, allowing partners to let out of their feelings without fear of retribution.

Behavioral approaches view conflicts as the result of how partners manage rewards and punishments. To improve communication from this perspective, couples should focus on positive reinforcement and constructive feedback. Instead of reacting to behaviors with criticism or withdrawal, couples should aim to acknowledge and appreciate each other's efforts. Implementing clear, fair, and consistent responses to each other's behavior can help reduce misunderstandings and build a more supportive environment. Setting aside regular time to discuss behaviors and their impacts can also enhance mutual understanding and cooperation.

Cognitive psychology attributes conflicts to irrational expectations and misunderstandings. To address this, couples should work on identifying and challenging unrealistic demands or cognitive distortions. Developing open and honest conversations about each other's expectations and perceptions can help clear misunderstandings. Strategies such as active listening and reflective communication can ensure that both partners feel heard and understood. Couples can improve communication and reduce the frequency and intensity of conflicts by clarifying intentions and addressing misconceptions.

COMPROMISE IN CONFLICT RESOLUTION

Compromise and flexibility are crucial for resolving conflict in relationships. If partners fail to acknowledge their mistakes fully, they are unlikely to resolve issues effectively. It's important to recognize that compromise often involves both gains and losses for each partner, but feeling understood and respected is crucial.

Prioritizing problem-solving through compromise over simply being right is vital for relationship success. Those who struggle with accountability and empathy are more likely to experience conflicts that undermine their relationship. Instead of competing over who has it harder or who contributes more, partners should focus on understanding each other and finding common ground.

Being open-minded and willing to embrace differences can lead to constructive conflict resolution, a critical factor in enhancing marital satisfaction. Conflict, though challenging, can be transformative and an opportunity for growth if approached with respect and a collaborative mindset. Effective conflict resolution strengthens the relationship, fosters trust, and improves communication. It's about resolving and using the conflict to grow and strengthen the relationship.

Constructive conflict resolution involves addressing disagreements in a way that both partners find fulfilling, contributing to ongoing marital satisfaction. In contrast, destructive conflict exacerbates issues and fosters negativity. A change in perspective, honest communication, and a foundation of love are critical for resolving conflicts constructively and maintaining a healthy relationship. Being open-minded, willing to compromise, and embracing differences contributes to constructive conflict resolution, which fosters marital satisfaction.

RESPECT IN CONFLICT RESOLUTION

Effective conflict resolution hinges on respecting your spouse, even in the heat of anger, hurt, or disappointment. Conflicts remain unresolved when respect is set aside, leading to further issues and emotional turmoil. Respect is crucial because it nurtures love and strengthens the bond between partners. Engaging in respectful communication fosters support and understanding, which are needed for resolving disagreements effectively. Remember, respect is not a luxury in conflict resolution; it's a necessity.

To navigate conflicts successfully, it's important to focus on the problem rather than fixating on mistakes or frustrations. Concentrating on the issue at hand enables you to address and resolve it collaboratively. Remember: as a married couple, you are a team, not adversaries. By focusing on the problem, you can work together to find a solution, strengthening your bond and relationship.

Research shows that partners who work through their problems grow stronger and more affectionate. This growth is possible only if both parties maintain respect for each other throughout the process. Mutual respect is the cornerstone of a secure and committed relationship. Avoid crossing the boundary with disrespectful behavior, no matter how intense the emotions are. Respect is the crucial thread connecting you when other relationship aspects seem exhausted. Fight fairly and wisely; always remember that your relationship matters and that mutual respect can resolve problems.

Avoid invalidating your spouse's arguments, emotions, viewpoints, or thought processes during conflict resolution. Patience and careful listening are vital. Allow your spouse to express themselves fully before jumping to conclusions. This approach ensures that your spouse feels heard and understood and fosters a sense of value and respect in the relationship. It is crucial to take turns speaking while being mindful of your tone, demeanor, and body language. Remember that once words are spoken, they cannot be taken back. Despite your feelings, avoid using hurtful or damaging language.

Respect should never wane in your relationship. It is the backbone of your partnership and should always be maintained. Even when trust, love, or temper may falter, never let respect slip away, especially during conflicts. This is when respect is needed the most. Maintaining respect is indispensable every day, in every situation.

Understanding that communication is nuanced and evolves gradually is key to maintaining peace of mind within a relationship. Sometimes, trying different approaches to communication might not yield immediate results. It is important not to become discouraged by these setbacks. Building effective communication with your spouse is gradual, and occasional challenges are typical. Everyone faces communication issues from time to time, especially with their spouse. Struggling in this area is perfectly normal, and you shouldn't feel bad about it.

You'll improve over time if you're willing to learn and stay determined. Communication isn't something that becomes perfect overnight. It takes patience and persistence. If you're committed to understanding and adapting, you'll gradually become a better communicator with your spouse. With all its ups and downs, this journey is part of growing together and strengthening your relationship. As Nyark and Hope assert, "For a unique and sustainable relationship in marriage, couples should enhance their relationship by understanding and applying relational communication skills to each other."[89]

MANAGE EMOTIONS CONSTRUCTIVELY

Managing emotions constructively is crucial for effective communication and conflict resolution in relationships. As emotional

---

89. Aniekan Nyark and Mark M. Hope, "Impact of Effective Communication in a Marriage," *International Journal of Research in Education, Science and Technology* 4, no. 2 (2022): 1-8, https://www.globalacademicstar.com/download/article/impact-of-effective-communication-in-a-marriage-81830.pdf.

beings, our feelings can often interfere with clear and productive dialogue. It's smart to choose the right moments to discuss issues rather than addressing conflicts daily, which can overwhelm the relationship. When emotions take over, it becomes difficult to resolve conflicts, and couples who struggle with emotional regulation often face ongoing issues.

Learning to manage and control emotions is vital, especially when they disrupt the functioning of the marriage. Emotions are natural responses to daily events, but a constant expression of negative feelings can be harmful rather than helpful. Instead of reporting every emotional upset, which can create more tension, addressing issues thoughtfully and when both partners are calm is more constructive.

Effective emotional management involves recognizing when feelings are clouding judgment and taking steps to address them appropriately. This might include waiting for a more suitable time to discuss sensitive topics, practicing self-regulation techniques, and focusing on problem-solving rather than venting frustrations. By maintaining emotional balance and choosing the right moments for communication, couples can improve their conflict resolution skills and enhance the overall health of their relationship.

BASIC CUES IN CONFLICT RESOLUTION

Understanding non-verbal cues and body language can aid in connecting with our spouse and fostering understanding in communication. However, each spouse should strive to express their feelings, needs, and expectations clearly and openly to their partner rather than expecting them to guess. Failing to do so would be unfair to one's spouse and could increase frustration and despair. As Tesser argues, "Nonobservable traits are much harder to verify for people than they are for objects… It is harder to verify what people are really like than what objects are really like."[90]

When addressing problems, providing context can assist each participant in understanding the conversation. In conflict resolution, some individuals present vague, imprecise arguments and bring up past grievances indiscriminately. The key is to concentrate on one issue at a time. Address one matter thoroughly and save discussions on other topics for another occasion. Avoiding clutter in the conversation prevents unresolved situations from arising.

Selfishness exists within everyone to varying degrees. When we receive a message from our spouse, we interpret it based on how relevant we perceive it to be to ourselves. Essentially, our connection to the message is determined by what we perceive as beneficial. We may become disinterested or restless if we don't sense our interests being addressed in the message. As Baumeister and Finkel avow, "Perhaps the most important determinant of a person's motivation to process a message is its perceived personal relevance. Whenever the message can be linked to some aspect of the message recipient's 'self,' it becomes more personally relevant and more likely to be processed."[91]

No matter how well you articulate your ideas, if your spouse is not predisposed to listen, he or she will not receive your message. Finding what touches their heart, however, may provoke a positive reception of the message. As Baumeister and Finkel advise, "The success of a persuasive attempt depends in part on whether the attitudes of

90. Abraham Tesser, "The Self in Social Psychology," in *Handbook of Social Psychology*, ed. Daniel T. Gilbert, Susan T. Fiske, and Gardner Lindzey, 2nd ed. (New York: McGraw-Hill, 1998), 413.

91. Roy F. Baumeister and Eli J. Finkel, *Advanced Social Psychology: The State of the Science* (New York: Oxford University Press, 2010), 314.

the recipients are modified in the desired direction. Designing appropriate strategies for attitude change depends on understanding the basic mechanisms underlying persuasion."[92]

How we approach the opening of a conversation with our spouse can either encourage or deter them from sharing their intended concerns or messages. It's crucial to prevent anything that could hinder productive conversations at all costs to maintain healthy connections with our spouse. As Baumeister and Finkel say, "Just as enhanced confidence in thoughts leads to greater reliance on them, increased doubt leads people to discard their thoughts. Sometimes, people might be so doubtful of their thoughts that they think the opposite is true. In such cases, doubt can lead to reversed effects with positive thoughts leading to less positive attitudes than negative thoughts."[93]

Mutual understanding between partners is crucial for marital satisfaction, with each individual needing to grasp this concept. Given the interdependence between partners and the potential differences in expectations, goals, and needs, it's important to devise strategies and goals that incorporate compromise, flexibility, and acceptance.

As mentioned before, selfish tendencies exist in all of us to varying degrees. When our needs and wants go unfulfilled, our communication might be influenced and obscured by our selfish inclinations. It's crucial to learn how to adapt and avoid resorting to feelings of resentment, disrespect, rejection, suppression, violence, or hatred. This approach can lead to profound satisfaction and greater success overall. Unfortunately, in today's world, patience is often viewed as a sign of weakness or an outdated mindset.

---

92. Ibid.

93. Ibid.

STRATEGIZE/THINK AHEAD
OF TIME AND ANTICIPATE

Before engaging in problem-solving discussions with your spouse, it's crucial to take some time to prepare. Analyze the situation thoroughly and develop a diplomatic approach to minimize potential misunderstandings and misinterpretations during the conversation. Adequate preparation involves thinking ahead and strategizing to mitigate possible misperceptions and miscommunication. This step is vital for building a good plan to address the situation more clearly and constructively.

For instance, understanding your spouse's personal attitudes and reactions to specific topics can significantly inform your approach. Anticipate their responses and put yourself in their position emotionally and mentally. If your spouse reacts strongly to recurring issues such as household responsibilities, parenting styles, financial matters, or personal insecurities, begin the conversation with appreciation. Identify and acknowledge at least two or three things they excel at, and express gratitude for these qualities.

It's important to avoid starting the conversation with blame or accusations. Instead, begin by expressing empathy and understanding. For example, you might say, "I understand where you're coming from and how challenging this situation can be. I'm not here to blame or judge you; I want us to have a productive conversation and work together on finding solutions." This approach helps in making the discussion more collaborative and less confrontational.

Ask questions like, "What can I do to help improve or get better at this particular issue?" By phrasing your concerns this way, you share the responsibility and emphasize that resolving the issue is a team effort. This approach reassures your spouse that you are committed to mutual satisfaction and are actively participating in finding solutions. Ending the conversation with a clear plan and reiterating your appreciation can reinforce positive communication and teamwork.

Couples must identify the root cause of conflict. Disagreements often arise from differing interests or unmet expectations. To resolve conflicts effectively, it is important to choose the right moment to discuss sensitive topics and respectfully convey your message. Ensuring both partners are engaged and actively participating is crucial for productive dialogue.

Successful communication begins with identifying shared interests as a foundation for discussion. This approach encourages both partners to contribute to the conversation actively.

Without engagement from both sides, effective communication becomes challenging. Focusing on common ground and clearly expressing your emotions and needs can facilitate a more productive and empathetic dialogue.

Strategizing and thinking ahead before addressing conflicts with your spouse can significantly enhance the effectiveness of your discussions. By preparing thoroughly, starting with appreciation, sharing responsibility, and focusing on common interests, you lay the groundwork for more constructive and collaborative problem-solving. Choose your words carefully and present your case respectfully to ensure the conversation remains productive and positive.

COMMUNICATE
OPENLY AND HONESTLY

Honesty and frankness can be particularly challenging when addressing hard truths with your spouse, especially on sensitive topics like personal insecurities, body weight, financial issues, or character flaws.

Speaking openly about these issues can be difficult, and many of us struggle with it. I find it hard to be completely honest about sensitive and complex matters, as they often touch on deep insecurities and fears.

When dealing with tough topics in a marriage, the situation is often complicated by a reluctance to bring up these issues for fear of causing emotional harm, damaging self-esteem, or disrupting peace and quiet. Many couples, particularly men, prefer to avoid these conversations entirely to maintain harmony and peace. They may choose to keep the peace rather than confront issues directly, believing that silence is the best course of action in the short term.

However, avoiding tough conversations in marriage might be detrimental to your marriage health. Ignoring or avoiding sensitive topics can lead to unresolved issues and internal hurt. No subject should be off-limits or considered taboo. Partners who avoid addressing their problems constructively may deal with unspoken grievances and emotional wounds, leading to a lack of fulfillment in their relationship.

When discussing complex topics, it's crucial to approach each other with love, care, respect, and grace. As mentioned earlier, starting these conversations with appreciation and empathy can pave the way for a more productive dialogue. Developing the habit of addressing all topics openly fosters healthy communication and contributes to a more satisfying and harmonious marriage. Avoiding discussions only perpetuates fear and dissatisfaction.

For a marriage to thrive, both partners must feel free to express their feelings and opinions openly, fear-free of negative repercussions or retaliation. Healthy communication involves both partners being able to discuss their expectations and emotions openly but in a loving, respectful, and constructive way. This openness is required for a balanced relationship.

Augsburger arguably and boldly explains how one can accomplish such a daunting challenge lovingly and successfully:

> Care-fronting is offering genuine caring that lifts, supports, and encourages the other. (To care is to bid another to grow, to welcome, invite, and support growth in another.) Care-fronting is being upfront with important facts that can call out new awareness, insight, and understanding. (To confront effectively is to offer the maximum of useful information with the minimum of threat and stress.) Care-fronting is loving and level conversation. It unites the love one has for the other with the honest truth that I am able to see about the two of us. Care-fronting unifies concern for relationship with concerns for goals—my goals, your goals, our goals. So one can have something to stand for (goals) as well as someone to stand with (relationship) without sacrificing one for the other or collapsing one into another. This allows each of us to be genuinely loving without giving away our power to think, choose, and act. In such honesty, one can love powerfully and be powerfully loving. These are not contradictory. They are complementary. (The opposite is to express powerless love until anger erupts in loveless power—to yield in pseudo-love until one overloads to the breaking point and then explodes with demands heated to the boiling point.).[94]

Communicating honestly and openly is important for a healthy

---

94. David Augsburger, *Caring Enough to Confront: How to Understand and Express Your Deepest Feelings toward Others* (Grand Rapids: Baker Publishing Group, 2009), 10, http://cdn. baker-publishinggroup.com/processed/bookresources/files/Excerpt_9780800729189.pdf?1512678628.

and fulfilling marriage. Confronting complex topics with care and respect while avoiding taboo subjects helps prevent internal hurt and promotes mutual understanding. By creating a safe space for honest expression, both partners can address issues constructively and build a stronger, more supportive relationship. The willingness and openness to give up parts of our interest to meet halfway is a good starting point for conflict resolution. Tension, clash, anger, and even hatred will rise if no effort on our part is being deployed to accommodate.

In the short term, opting not to deal with issues with care may help pacify an angry partner; however, in the long run, Augsburger's "carefronting" is the most beneficial approach to conflict resolution. If you opt to withdraw, avoid confrontation issues, and endure, the issue may appear resolved momentarily, but it might not withstand dissatisfaction in the future, potentially leading to tension later on. Eventually, you may feel compelled to give up.

Therefore, it's advisable to "carefront" your spouse. Augsburger breaks it down this way: of the five options in conflict situations— (1) I win–you lose; (2) I want out, I'll withdraw; (3) I'll give in for good relations; (4) I'll meet you halfway; (5) I can care and confront—the last is the most effective, the most truly loving, the most growth-promoting for human relationships.[95]

Engaging in carefronting leads to growth, transformation, intimacy, authentic connection, trust, comfort, security, recommitment, and ultimately, fulfillment. Augsburger puts it better this way, "The two arms of a genuine relationship are: truth reaches out to touch truth; love embraces love. The authenticity, honesty, and transparency of truthfulness build trusting relationship; the positive regard

---

95. Ibid., 20.

of warmth that is not possessive offers affirmation. Confronting and caring stimulate growth."[96]

In this chapter, we've explored the subtleties and complexities of communication, recognizing that it's far from being a one-size-fits-all solution for effective marital communication. Discovering the right approach to communicate effectively with your spouse is a valuable investment of time and dedication. Each couple crafts its own unique story, shaped by individual experiences and circumstances, yet with commonalities among them. Given our differences, it's rational to identify a communication style that aligns with our lifestyle and meets the needs of both partners.

Embrace the process of learning and growth. As you do your best to strive to enhance your communication skills with your spouse, you'll be amazed by the positive outcomes. The key is to create a nurturing communicative environment where open dialogue thrives, devoid of fear, anger, suppression, hatred, or division. Make it your mission to cultivate a healthy marriage with your spouse, drawing inspiration from Christ's perfect and exemplary model for all believers. Remember, there's always potential for growth and improvement in your communication, offering hope and optimism for the future of your relationship.

---

96. Ibid., 20.

CHAPTER VII

PROTECTING YOUR MARRIAGE

Protecting the marriage bed is paramount to a healthy union. When entering marriage, we often envision a partnership filled with honesty, openness, loyalty, and fulfillment. However, unforeseen wounds such as unfaithfulness can arise. No marriage is immune to the challenge of infidelity, regardless of maturity, spirituality, strength, or preparedness.

In the face of unfaithfulness, does this spell the end of the union? Is it feasible to heal from the emotional and mental anguish and forge ahead? Are there measures to prevent affairs? Can a marriage endure such betrayal? The resounding answer is yes. Numerous marriages have weathered the storm of infidelity and emerged stronger and happier. It is indeed possible for your marriage to thrive once more. As long as hope persists, there is potential for restoration. Remember, healing is possible.

In this chapter, we will discover types of unfaithfulness, analyze causes and consequences, develop ways to prevent them, and discuss how to move on from their hurt. We will also examine how to heal from an affair from the perspective of God's truth.

FORMS OF MARITAL INFIDELITY

Marital infidelity, a complex issue, can manifest in diverse ways and present itself in various forms and guises. Understanding these types of infidelity, whether physical, financial, material, or emotional, can equip you with the knowledge to recognize and address them should they arise in your relationship. The most recognized form is engaging in physical intimacy with someone other than one's spouse.

It can assume several manifestations: physical, financial, material, and emotional. Emotional affairs can encompass emotions such as longing, detachment (failing to exhibit the love or care expected in the relationship), and emotional attachment to someone outside the marriage. Financial infidelity involves a lack of transparency, such as concealing assets from one's spouse.

McBain and Fuller articulate that when a violation or breach of fidelity occurs in a relationship, it usually falls under a specific category. Categories or types of infidelity include physical infidelity, emotional cheating, cyber infidelity, object infidelity, and financial infidelity. Here are seven types of infidelity:

Physical infidelity: Physical or sexual connection outside of the relationship. There may or may not be an emotional component between partners.

Emotional infidelity: Emotional attachment or intimacy with another person. Emotional affairs, often overlooked, can be as damaging, if not more, to a relationship as a physical affair.

The emotional bond that is broken can be difficult to repair, and the trust that is shattered can take a long time to rebuild.

Cyber infidelity: Social media has made it easier for people to engage in online messages, chats, forums, or groups with sexual content. Cyber infidelity also includes viewing erotic stimuli, such as cheating via pornography.

Object infidelity: An obsession or interest outside of the relationship can result in what is known as an object affair. This is a situation where one partner is more focused on something such as work or their phone, which causes a distraction from the relationship.

Financial infidelity: Money can become a point of contention for many relationships. If it progresses to the point of financial infidelity, one partner may be deceitful about how much money they earn, how they earn money, how much debt they owe, and how they spend or loan out money. They may even have money hidden away in cash or other bank accounts that their partner doesn't know about.

Micro cheating: A term for actions that bother a partner, such as flirting that crosses a line, but there is no intention of straying outside of the relationship.

Combined infidelity: When the infidelity includes more than one type. Many infidelities include elements of both sexual and emotional intimacies. A cyber affair may also be considered a form of emotional infidelity.[97]

---

97. Tristan McBain and Kristen Fuller, "Infidelity: Types, Causes, and Effects," *Choosing Therapy*, October 4, 2022, https://www.choosingtherapy.com/infidelity/.

CAUSES OF MARITAL BETRAYAL

When an affair arises, it signifies an underlying issue within the relationship that requires attention. Typically, this issue has been present but unaddressed before the affair. Often, this problem acts as an impediment to the growth of the marital relationship. Individuals unwilling to pursue growth and accustomed to the status quo may avoid investing the necessary effort to resolve the stagnant issue, potentially leading to unfaithfulness. One or both partners may be aware of the problem but choose to deny, resist, dismiss, or postpone addressing it, eventually resulting in an affair.

Various factors can contribute to extramarital sex. Among the most common are marital discontentment and dissatisfaction, a decline in emotional connection with one's spouse, ineffective communication, a lack of accountability and planning, diminished commitment to the marriage, a lack of shared life goals, self-centeredness, negligence or disregard, a lack of self-restraint, a desire to validate one's worth, or a lack of self-assurance. Additionally, disloyalty may stem from sexual dissatisfaction, ongoing unresolved conflicts leading to constant arguments that accumulate without resolution, and poor conflict resolution skills.

Another contributing factor may be the lack of support from one partner toward the dreams, life goals, and aspirations of the other. This could prompt the affected individual to seek support elsewhere, eventually leading to adultery. Recognizing the importance of being each other's primary supporters and advocating for the other's dreams is crucial. Everyone needs positive support and validation, not criticism. This mutual support can solidify the bond and reduce the likelihood of infidelity.

Other contributing factors leading to infidelity include prioritizing the opinions of outsiders over your spouse's, which can strain your marriage. Remember, your commitment is to your spouse, not to external influences. Over-sharing with friends, family, or colleagues can inadvertently open the door to manipulation and extramarital affairs. It's urgent to limit disclosing intimate details to anyone outside your marriage and address concerns directly with your spouse to foster intimacy and resilience.

Additionally, withholding sexual intimacy as a form of manipulation or coercion can drive a partner to seek fulfillment elsewhere, leading to unfaithfulness. Neglecting your spouse's sexual needs is selfish and detrimental to the relationship. Fulfilling your marital duties with love and consideration is crucial to maintaining trust and fidelity.

Mismanagement of finances and disagreements over money matters can also strain a marriage and potentially lead to cheating. Open communication and mutual agreement on financial decisions are vital to prevent marital discord. Failing to adhere to agreed-upon financial plans can create tension and drive a spouse to seek solace or guidance outside the marriage.

Furthermore, neglecting to seek assistance when facing marital challenges can contribute to disloyalty. Some issues require professional intervention or support from trusted individuals who have your marriage's best interests at heart. It's wise to seek help from qualified professionals or supportive friends and family members who respect your relationship and can offer constructive advice.

In seeking help, it's crucial to be discerning and avoid counsel from those who may undermine your marriage or lack the necessary experience. Choosing the right sources of support can make a significant difference in navigating marital difficulties and safeguarding the integrity of your relationship.

CONSEQUENCES OF
MARITAL UNFAITHFULNESS

The repercussions of extramarital relations are far-reaching and can inflict immense pain, anguish, and damage on those involved, including the betrayed, the betrayer, and their broader social circle, such as children, friends, and family members. Betrayal leaves a profound and lasting impact, causing deep emotional distress and upheaval.

Marissa Moore argues that you might experience symptoms consistent with post-traumatic stress. Instead of a shock to your system, as with post-traumatic stress disorder (PTSD), discovering cheating can be a mental shock to the system you've built as a couple. Research shows that infidelity can also cause increased anxiety and depression, in addition to stress.[98] She adds that infidelity can have lasting impacts on partners and children involved. Grief, brain changes, behaviors down the road, and mental health conditions such as anxiety, chronic stress, and depression can result.[99]

The consequences of unfaithfulness can manifest across various dimensions, including emotional, mental, financial, psychological, and physical realms. Some outcomes may include diminished self-confidence and self-esteem, heightened depression, marital dissolution, resentment towards the offending party's gender, reluctance to forgive, decreased productivity at work, emotional distress, and disillusionment with romantic relationships. As Castro-Bofill et al. explain, "Having parental infidelity threatens the foundation of the marriage as well as the whole family relationship. It affects the relationship of the child to

---

98. Marissa Moore, "Long-Term Psychological Effects of Infidelity," *PsychCentral*, October 29, 2021, Accessed April 21, 2024, https://psychcentral.com/health/long-term-psychological -effects-of-infidelity.

99. Ibid.

couples not only emotionally but physically, mentally, and socially as well which may also influence the establishment of the former's relationships. It is a problem which has consequences that permanently damage the parent-child relationship as well as other future relationships."[100]

STRATEGIES FOR SAFEGUARDING MARITAL TRUST AND COMMITMENT

The most effective strategy for maintaining romantic fidelity in committed relationships is proactive prevention. By addressing potential issues beforehand, the risk of adultery can be significantly reduced or eliminated altogether. Married partners should confront any existing concerns, whether minor or major before they escalate and potentially result in damaging consequences like an affair. Ignoring, denying, rejecting, or trivializing marital issues only exacerbates problems over time. Open and continuous communication between spouses is critical, as assuming that issues will resolve themselves is not sustainable.

Vowels and Mark discovered ways to prevent infidelity: These results suggest that intervening in relationships when difficulties first arise may be the best way to prevent future infidelity. Furthermore, because sexual desire was one of the most robust predictors of infidelity, discussing sexual needs and desires and finding ways to meet those needs in relationships may also decrease the risk of infidelity.[101]

Marriage counselors, therapists, religious scholars, and spiritual leaders propose various ways to prevent adultery from happening.

---

100. Francine Rose A. de Castro-Bofill et al., "Living within a Broken Vow: The Impact of Parental Infidelity among Late Adolescents in Establishing Romantic Relationships," *Universal Journal of Psychology* 4, no. 5 2016): 228-235, DOI: 10.13189/ujp.2016.040503.

101. Laura M. Vowels, Matthew J. Vowels and Kristen P. Mark, "Is Infidelity Predictable?: Using Explainable Machine Learning to Identify the Most Important Predictors of Infidelity," *The Journal of Sex Research* 59, no. 2 (2022): 224-237, DOI: 10.1080/00224499.2021.1967846.

Exequiel Gono, Jr. suggests that "Rebuilding trust and addressing the aftermath of cheating necessitate open communication, commitment to emotional connection, and, in some cases, seeking professional help through couples counseling."[102]

Here are several recommendations I propose to prevent marital affairs.

Devote Genuine Attention to Your Marriage Every Day

This entails avoiding complacency, treating your marital bond with utmost seriousness, and investing consistent effort and dedication into its upkeep. Protect it vigilantly through every available means and steer clear of evil counsel. Refrain from bargaining your spouse's worth to those in your social circle. Elevate your spouse to the highest priority—demonstrate respect, nurture, and cherish them above all others, including children, parents, and siblings. Your spouse must perceive and acknowledge the depth of your esteem for them surpassing anyone else's.

Pledge Unwavering Commitment to Your Marriage for a Lifetime

When your commitment serves as the solid foundation of your relationship, it can withstand life's challenges. On the other hand, starting your relationship on shaky, false, or unfounded principles will likely lead to its downfall.

Right from the Start of Your Romantic Relationship, Openly Discuss Your Sexual Expectations and Desire

This is crucial. It's a step that should be taken before marriage, often during pre-marriage counseling or through intimate discussions

---

102. Exequiel R. Gono, Jr., "Model of Cheating in a Romantic Relationship," *European Journal of Social Sciences Studies*, 9, 5, 2024, DOI: 10.46827/ejsss.v9i5.1650.

between just the two of you regarding your sexual preferences, expectations, and desires for pleasurable intimacy. Pose questions such as: What specific touches please you? What aspects of my body do you find appealing? How can I maintain attractiveness for you? What actions or behaviors are turn-offs for you?

Be specific in Your Inquiries and Openly Express Your Own Preferences to Your Spouse without Hesitation, Reservation, or Fear of Negative Consequences

This aspect of communication should prioritize honesty, employing straightforward, plain, and easily understandable language. Avoid expecting your spouse to know your preferences intuitively.

Set Boundaries and Expectations

Anticipate potential issues and define parameters together. Customize boundaries to align with your relationship's unique needs and desires. Clearly communicate these boundaries to each other and, most importantly, adhere to them.

Guard against Forming Emotional Attachments to Individuals to Whom You're Sexually Attracted

Emotional bonds can develop subtly with regular acquaintances such as coworkers, friends, or even random encounters. Be wary, as these connections can arise unexpectedly. If you find yourself developing feelings for someone other than your spouse, address and dismiss them immediately. Refrain from entertaining such thoughts or emotions, as they significantly threaten your marriage. While experiencing feelings is natural, unfaithfulness only materializes when these emotions are nurtured and allowed to grow. Take proactive steps to eliminate these thoughts and safeguard your marriage from harm.

Resist Temptation

Recognize your personal limitations, vulnerabilities, and boundaries and establish clear boundaries you will not cross. Avoid flirtatious behavior, which may signal openness to romantic or sexual advances. Temptation can arise unexpectedly and escalate rapidly, so exercise caution and avoid situations that may facilitate it. Be vigilant and proactive in steering clear of compromising circumstances.

Reignite the Flame of Your Dying Love

Life and romantic relationships are dynamic. Without effort and care, love can dwindle. Even in the face of waning affection, couples can discover ways to rekindle the passion they once shared, thereby averting the temptation of an affair. Allowing love to wither increases the likelihood of seeking fulfillment elsewhere.

Value and Acknowledge one Another's Worth

Expressing appreciation is recommended. It's crucial to cultivate a habit of speaking positively to each other. Recognize the admirable qualities in your spouse, no matter how small they may seem, and express your gratitude. Appreciate the decision your spouse made to marry you. Regularly acknowledge their dedication, affection, and contributions to the family's welfare.

Guard against Complacency

As previously mentioned, avoid taking each other for granted. Sustaining love demands ongoing effort—a commitment that knows no end. The moment complacency sets in, so does the bond erosion between you. Choose to remain together, not out of obligation but from genuine affection.

Foster Open and Sincere Communication

Often, deficient communication skills can inflict more damage to your marriage than anticipated. Enhance your communication with your spouse to mitigate potential issues. Inadequate conflict resolution can breed frustration, discontent, and emotional distance. Encourage a healthy communication dynamic where both parties feel empowered to express their emotions, fears, needs, expectations, goals, and desires respectfully and affectionately without withholding significant concerns.

The fear of upsetting one's partner, escalating conflicts, or being misunderstood, ridiculed, dismissed, or rejected often hinders married couples from communicating openly, clearly, and honestly. Difficulty in expressing oneself candidly and feeling heard signifies underlying problems. These communication barriers can negatively impact marital well-being, even without involving cheating. Thus, developing communication marked by compassion, sincerity, and understanding is crucial.

Underline the Importance of Spending Quality Time Together

Therapists, counselors, and marriage specialists agree that quality time improves and increases intimacy between couples. However, people may perceive or define quality time differently. Regardless, figure out what qualifies as quality time for your spouse and try to spend some together, either just the two of you or as a family. It can be vacationing, playing games, and going to a movie theater. Remember:

nurturing your relationship through quality time is a key to preventing and recovering from infidelity.

Engage in Daily Prayer and Bible Reading Together

Studies show that couples who spend time reading the Bible and praying together often growing closer, reducing the risk of harm to their marriage. They conscientiously strive to avoid intentionally hurting each other and seek to uphold God's principles, steering clear of actions that would bring shame to His name. If you and your family don't currently read the Bible together or pray regularly, consider making time for it. You'll likely notice a positive impact right away.

Support Each Other's Personal Dreams and Ambitions Actively

Resist the temptation to dismiss, belittle, reject, or ignore your spouse's dreams. Dreams provide purpose and vitality to our lives; existence can feel dull without them. As a partner, it's vital to prioritize supporting your spouse's aspirations and aiding them in achieving their goals. This supportive stance serves as a protective barrier for your marriage. When spouses feel supported, understood, and valued, the inclination to seek solace outside the relationship diminishes significantly.

Exercise Caution When Sharing Details of Your Marriage with Others

Sharing intimate details with individuals, especially in the absence of your spouse, can foster emotional connections that may lead to extramarital sex. Be mindful not to overshare, as doing so can inadvertently pave the way for inappropriate emotional attachments. While it's acceptable to discuss certain everyday matters, refrain from divulging specific details, particularly those of a negative nature. Use discretion and wisdom in your sharing practices. Not doing so can lead to a breakdown in trust and emotional distance in your marriage.

HEALING AND REBUILDING
FROM MARITAL BETRAYAL

Various approaches (express expectations clearly, adopt open and honest communication, learn to forgive and let go, and use external resources as needed) can be employed to navigate the pain of moving forward from the hurt caused by a marital affair. Both partners must be committed to resolving the issue together. The offending party must take responsibility for their actions, acknowledge their faults, commit to avoiding recurrence, sincerely seek forgiveness, and forgive themselves. Rebuilding trust will require significant effort. It will take faith and resilience from the offended to heal and rebuild, but this will take time and effort. Implementing these strategies in your relationship today is strongly encouraged.

Not rushing into decisions is brilliant, as hasty choices can harm the marriage or personal well-being. Avoid hastily jumping to conclusions following a recent discovery; allow time for processing and healing. Engage trusted individuals in your support network as necessary. Remain open and receptive to forgiveness, regardless of the extent of your pain. Avoid shutting down constructive communication channels.

Both partners need to engage in deep discussions about these issues: If reconciliation is desired and you aim to preserve your marriage, it is imperative to establish a forgiveness strategy. The aggrieved party bears the weighty responsibility of granting forgiveness, while the offending party must commit to avoiding a repeat of their transgression and demonstrate a genuine behavior change. A comprehensive plan must be clearly outlined for both parties, and expectations must be redefined.

Forgiveness can be particularly challenging in such circumstances. However, when forgiveness is extended, it can unlock new depths of love within your marriage that were previously unexplored. Forgiveness has the transformative power to free you from the grip of anger, mental anguish, emotional distress, and psychological turmoil. The potency of forgiveness transcends mere words.

Here are ways and strategies you can heal and rebuild from a marriage affair:

Express Expectations Openly, Clearly, and Honestly

Expectations represent the new standards or guidelines agreed upon by both partners as you move forward. In situations where one partner has transgressed, they must refrain from defensiveness, acknowledge wrongdoing, and agree to the new terms established together. No topics should be deemed too weighty, inflexible, or off-limits for discussion. These so-called "forbidden topics," which could include financial issues, sexual problems, or personal insecurities, should be addressed in regular conversations without fear. Failure to discuss certain issues may exacerbate them, potentially leading to disloyalty. Approach all discussions with clarity, directness, and honesty while maintaining mutual respect.

Improve Your Overall Competence in Communication

When communication breaks down, all other aspects eventually follow suit. It's crucial to dismantle any barriers hindering healthy communication between both partners. Make a safe environment where everyone expresses their thoughts, desires, and expectations respectfully and lovingly, without fear of negative reactions or harsh consequences. Enhance your communication skills to ensure no taboo topics, pretense, dishonesty, or obstacles impede open dialogue.

For instance, if your partner expresses discomfort with you divulging marital secrets to outsiders, including family members, listen without becoming defensive. Instead of justifying your actions based on familial closeness, acknowledge their concerns. Similarly, if one partner struggles with an addiction, such as gambling, it's elementary not to respond defensively by justifying the behavior based on financial autonomy. Instead, strive to understand your partner's perspective and address the issue collaboratively.

Weight loss can be another sensitive topic in marriages. If discussing certain subjects freely and respectfully proves challenging, it indicates a communication issue that needs attention. If your partner expresses discomfort with your weight gain, avoid defensiveness or feeling attacked. Instead, listen to their perspective and work together to devise a plan for weight management. Addressing such concerns can help maintain physical attraction and intimacy in the relationship. Playing the victim or deflecting blame will not alter the reality of your partner's feelings, potentially leading to emotional distance.

Find the Underlying Issue or Motivation that Pushed Your Spouse to Do It in the First Place

Please don't be harsh and unkind about it. You can be angry rightfully but remain respectful when trying to bottom up the cause of the problem. I can guarantee you that you may never learn the actual cause if you push hard with anger. What you will hear will be lies or unrelated excuses. But if you patiently take your time to learn and ask specific questions, you will have the answers you need. If you are unable to dig out the problem, as they say, "the same cause produces the same effect." It may happen again.

Learn to Manage Your Negative Feelings and Thoughts Effectively

Coping with these emotions after experiencing betrayal is undeniably challenging. However, mastering the ability to release negativity and cultivate positive thinking can lead to emotional, psychological, and even physical healing. Holding onto negative emotions will only deplete you emotionally, physically, and psychologically.

Embrace Patience as a Guiding Light

By navigating this experience with patience, you can uncover valuable lessons and grow personally and as a spouse. Resist the urge to rush your recovery or prematurely terminate your relationship. Remember: patience empowers individuals to achieve remarkable feats beyond their imagination.

Work on Rebuilding and Re-growing Trust

This is a gradual process, and until trust is restored, moving beyond the pain may prove difficult. Forgiveness is a crucial part of this process. It's not about forgetting or condoning the actions that led to the infidelity but about choosing to let go of the anger and resentment. Cultivating positive perceptions of your spouse is also essential to gradually rebuilding trust. Remember, patience and perseverance are vital to this journey.

Reestablish Sexual Intimacy, but Do so with Care and Patience

Allow yourself the necessary time to heal before attempting to reconnect sexually. Avoid completely shutting down sexual intimacy, as doing so may exacerbate feelings of disconnection and potentially lead to further instances of adultery.

Seek Support If Necessary

Don't hesitate to seek assistance from friends, family members, spiritual leaders, or professional counselors or therapists. Seeking external support during challenging times is not a sign of weakness but a recognition of the importance of navigating life's difficulties with assistance.

Remember You Are Not Alone

Many people faced similar challenges and successfully rebuilt happy marriages. By actively playing your part, you can hold onto hope and work towards the possibility of a brighter future. It is achievable.

FINDING FREEDOM IN LETTING GO

We're all human and have our limits and breaking points. If you find you can't forgive or endure the pain caused by betrayal, the only choice left may be to separate or divorce. You can't live a life filled with misery. The Lord tells us that His blessings come without sorrow. When your pain outweighs your joy, it's time to consider separation. God understands; He doesn't want you to suffer like this. Many have found new love and happiness afterward, and you shouldn't feel guilty for needing to move on from your spouse's infidelity.

Sometimes, despite your best efforts, things don't change. Some people's patterns of betrayal are ingrained and unlikely ever to change meaningfully. Please don't waste your energy and time trying to change them in such cases. Life is too short to chase after what can't be caught. Those who refuse to change are like the wind—you can't hold onto them no matter how hard you try. The best choice is to seek a life where you are respected, loved, and appreciated. God will bless your new journey and bring you joy again. But remember that this step comes after exhausting all options and still finding yourself unable to move on. God loves you, and He wants you to be happy. If it isn't working, don't force it. Rebuild your life and take charge of your own destiny.

BIBLICAL RECOMMENDATIONS

God established the institution of marriage and holds it in high regard. He provided principles and values for us to follow in our marriages to honor Him and find fulfillment in our relationships. However, we tend to stray from His guidelines more often than not. With the entrance of sin into the world, its effects have permeated our marriages as well, leading to infidelity and causing turmoil for couples. Regrettably, churches, like the Pharisees, often prioritize adherence to traditions over following God's principles.

In cases of infidelity, the immediate response that is often encouraged and considered is divorce. Everyone likes to quote Matthew 19:8: "Jesus replied, 'Moses permitted divorce only as a concession to your hard hearts, but it was not what God had originally intended. And I tell you this, whoever divorces his wife and marries someone else commits adultery—unless his wife has been unfaithful.'"

Is divorce truly what aligns with God's desires? Isn't there a more biblically grounded approach to addressing infidelity than simply resorting to separation? Forgiveness is undoubtedly challenging—it's often described as divine rather than human. Yet, who among us hasn't sought forgiveness at least once in our lives? Reflect on your own experiences of seeking forgiveness—how did it feel to need forgiveness? It's important to remember that feelings of guilt and shame are expected in these situations, but they should not define you or your marriage.

The Bible unequivocally asserts that nothing is beyond forgiveness. While it does mention divorce as permissible in cases of unfaithfulness, we should reflect on our own shortcomings and failures. Consider how often we have been unfaithful to God in our attitudes, actions, and thoughts. Reflect on how frequently we have neglected to share His message of salvation with others or failed to give Him the glory He deserves for His blessings in our lives. This self-examination highlights the need for humility and understanding when faced with issues of infidelity and reconciliation in our own relationships.

The Bible directs us toward repentance and grace when dealing with marital infidelity. Just as God was willing to reconcile with Israel if she repented and turned back to Him, we are called to extend grace and seek reconciliation in our own marriages when faced with betrayal. Genuine repentance is crucial; it is not merely about acknowledging wrongdoing but also about a sincere transformation of heart and behavior. This process reflects the grace God shows us daily and invites us to live out that same grace in our relationships.

If the betrayer truly repents, God can restore and renew what was broken, offering the chance for a new beginning in the relationship. However, if repentance is absent, Scripture, particularly 1 Corinthians 5, guides how to handle such situations. It emphasizes the importance of addressing unrepentant behavior with seriousness while maintaining the possibility of reconciliation for those who genuinely seek to mend their ways. In all cases, our approach should be rooted in the principles of forgiveness, grace, and a commitment to living out God's commands in our relationships.

God's perfect example of forgiveness should inspire each of us. Sending your one and only son to die for someone who wronged you wouldn't be my choice. But God did it for us when we were lost. He didn't withhold Christ, even though it was painful for Him to do it.

At times, moving forward seems impossible on your own, necessitating divine intervention. Seek God's assistance, beseeching Him for the wisdom, energy, strength, and discernment needed to extend forgiveness. Rely on His Holy Spirit for support and guidance as you navigate this challenging journey.

Bear in mind that your marriage can be preserved with your commitment and God's grace. While the adversary seeks to destroy, Christ offers abundant life. If God has blessed you with marriage, He will bestow His blessings upon it, as He highly esteems the institution of marriage.

Refuse to succumb to societal pressures, justified anger, or the influence of others urging you to end your marriage prematurely. Even in the face of apparent hopelessness, there remains the possibility of hope.

Throughout this section, we've discovered that married couples must protect their marriages at all costs. Fidelity must be pursued, and unfaithfulness avoided. Christ's perfect and admirable example of forgiveness and love should inspire every believer's marriage. We've acknowledged the challenges and temptations that threaten to undermine the sanctity of our marriage—whether through external pressures, past wounds, or the lure of selfish desires. Yet, in the face of these trials, we've discovered the power of God's grace—a grace that empowers us to resist temptation, heal brokenness, and cultivate intimacy that honors Him.

Our commitment to protecting our marriage bed extends beyond the confines of our bedroom. It's a daily choice to prioritize our spouse, cherish their heart, and honor our covenant before God. Carry the truth that our marriage bed is a sacred space where love is nurtured, passion is ignited, and God's presence is felt. It is a beautiful testament to the sanctity of marriage.

We must guard our marriage bed fiercely, tend it tenderly, and allow it to flourish as a testimony to the beauty of God's design for marriage. May the God who created us in His image, who knit us together in our mother's womb, and who delights in the intimacy of His children, continue to bless and protect our marriage bed, now and forevermore. Let us remain determined and committed to this sacred task.

CONCLUSION

Marriage is a sacred and dynamic institution that demands genuine care, commitment, and understanding. It should never be approached with lightheartedness or confusion. When entered into with adherence to God's divine principles, it brings profound joy, fulfillment, satisfaction, and a sense of security. However, those who approach it unprepared or casually may face pain, suffering, and regret beyond explanation.

A thriving married life is attainable if we respect its foundational rules. No one enters marriage fully equipped with all the knowledge needed, but by remaining flexible and willing to learn, we can grow into better partners for ourselves, our spouses, and our children. We have the power to be positive inspirations rather than negative ones—because negative influences can lead others astray. Strive to be the person who positively inspires others in their marriages.

You have the potential to create a marriage beyond your wildest dreams. Embrace the principles and values explored in this book; countless blessings await you. Don't let stubbornness, negligence, or pride stand in your way. Adopt a mindset of growth, transformation, and positivity, and you'll find yourself blessed beyond measure, exceeding all expectations and words.

In *Beyond Expectations: The Marriage You Hope For*, we've explored the depths of God's design for marriage—a design rooted in His established principles and values, love, guided by faith and hope, and sustained by His unfailing grace. Essential virtues such as selflessness, empathy, commitment, fidelity, understanding, effective communication, active listening, compassionate confrontation, mutual understanding, and a shared purpose are necessary for nurturing deeply fulfilling marriages.

Central to the book's message is recognizing that relationships are essential in God's eyes. It stresses that a marriage can only find true fulfillment and satisfaction by embracing God's presence, praying, obeying His guidance, and applying His principles. The book emphasizes the importance of making God the focal point of your marital union, advocating for the constant pursuit of His values and precepts.

Throughout this book, we've encountered the reality that marriage is not merely a human institution but a sacred covenant—a reflection of the divine love between Christ and His bride, the Church. It's a partnership forged in the fires of selflessness, humility, and sacrificial love—a partnership that invites us to emulate Christ's example of love for us.

Yet, we've also acknowledged the challenges and struggles accompanying this journey, which is marked by brokenness, imperfection, and the constant need for grace. But even in our weakness, we've discovered the transformative power of God's love, which heals wounds, restores hope, and breathes new life into our relationships.

Marriage is not a destination but a lifelong pilgrimage, a sacred dance of growth, discovery, and renewal. Hold fast to the hope that sustains us.

I hope that *Beyond Expectation* is a guiding light for couples everywhere, a beacon of hope in a world longing for love, and a roadmap for those seeking to build a marriage exceeding the basics and reaching for the extraordinary. With God, all things are possible. He who began good work in us will be faithful in completing it until the day of Christ Jesus.

Let us step boldly into the future with hearts full of faith, minds renewed by God's truth, and hands joined in love. For in God's perfect timing and by His abundant grace, the marriage we hope for awaits—beyond expectation, beyond imagination, beyond anything we could ask or comprehend.

ABOUT THE AUTHOR

Married with three children, Dr. W. Jeremie Ouedraogo and his wife Mary, have firsthand experience of the challenges and rewards of building a strong, healthy marriage and family. His personal journey, combined with his academic expertise, drives his dedication to promoting healthy, godly marriages that thrive over time.

Originally from Burkina Faso, West Africa, Dr. Ouedraogo has both non-western and western cultural experiences to draw from as he pursued his doctoral studies in Intercultural Studies. His research, focused on equipping couples to build God centered marriages.

Dr. Ouedraogo is also a Financial Planner with certifications as a Chartered Financial Consultant (ChFC), Chartered Life Underwriter (CLU), and a Masters degree in Business, bringing a wealth of experience in helping individuals and families secure their financial futures.

In addition to his professional accomplishments, Dr. Ouedraogo is deeply involved in his church, where he serves as a guest speaker and is a member of the leadership team. He and his wife, have been involved in several ministries, with a particular focus on building strong foundations in faith, relationships, and prayer life.